Praise for
How to Raise a Founder With Heart

"I've spent most of my life developing programs and founding ventures to help people surpass their self-imposed limits and realize their ultimate potential. It's a tremendous pleasure to read a book written for parents that will help them establish a mindset of problem-solving, empathy, and limitless potential in their children. Jim has nailed it. He weaves together his entrepreneurial background—including creating the LeapFrog LeapPad, one of the most successful educational products in history—and family experiences into a compelling book of stories, science, and parenting tips that are funny, poignant, and insightful. How to Raise a Founder With Heart *is a must-read."*
—*Tony Robbins, entrepreneur, philanthropist, bestselling author, and life and business strategist*

"The current generation of adults—us—is leaving the next generation—our own children and grandchildren—with some huge PTSs (problems to solve). Social problems include wars and poverty; science problems include global warming, cancer, dementia—and we still need to get to another planet. That's just the tip of the iceberg. The good news is that we're giving the next generation powerful microprocessor-based tools that no previous generation has had. That's why the timing of this different kind of parenting book is so important. How to Raise a Founder With Heart *reads more like a story-filled conversation with Jim Marggraff rather than a list of parenting directives, and it's full of helpful seed ideas that just might grow into some much-needed solutions."*
—*Warren Buckleitner, educational researcher and editor of* Children's Technology Review

"*Among the scores of entrepreneurs I met in 20 years of reporting on Silicon Valley for the* New York Times, Fortune, Forbes, *and other publications, Jim Marggraff always stood out. A serial inventor who created megahits like LeapFrog's LeapPad, a "talking" book that taught millions of children how to read, he always showed a knack for tackling real-world problems with ingenuity and a sense of purpose. In* How to Raise a Founder With Heart, *Jim has turned the lessons he learned along the way into a practical parenting guide focused on nurturing a child's problem-solving abilities. It's a timely book filled with actionable advice for parents who want to foster in their children the mindset of a "founder"—someone with the initiative and courage to tackle any problem, zero in on its essence, and solve it with a eye toward making a positive contribution.* How to Raise a Founder With Heart *is filled with stories from Jim's life as an entrepreneur and from his and his wife's, MJ, journey raising their children, Blake and Annie, that make it a delightful read.*"
—*Miguel Helft, former San Francisco bureau chief and technology editor at* Forbes

"*Overall, I think this book will appeal to many parents because of its insights, ideas, and encouragement to parents that they, too, can turn their kids into productive leaders and founders. The chapter on empathy is my favorite of all the chapters. Getting your kids to put themselves in others' shoes is a life-changer, when it works!*"
—*Randy Haykin, entrepreneur, angel investor, venture capitalist, and author*

"*I've been a business leader (but not a founder) at several successful children-oriented companies and had the pleasure of working closely with Jim as an entrepreneurial founder at LeapFrog. I always admired Jim for his brilliance and creativity, as well as for how he and his wife, MJ, raised their amazing children.* How to Raise a Founder With Heart *is a great guide for raising wonderful*

children. *It's a must-read for all parents and grandparents, but it's also extremely helpful to those engaged in business and anyone who is curious about improving their own lives and the lives of others. I highly recommend you give it a read.*"
—*Tom Kalinske, former* CEO *of Matchbox, Sega, and Mattel, and former* CEO *and chairman of LeapFrog*

"*This is a fascinating book. It will be very useful to its immediate audience—parents who want to help their children develop the healthiest intellectual, emotional, and moral habits for life—and it's also full of valuable insights and tips for a wide range of readers. I'm very glad that Jim Marggraff has shared the lessons of his business and family experiences.*"
—*James Fallows, national correspondent for* The Atlantic Monthly *and author of* Our Towns: A 100,000-Mile Journey Into the Heart of America

"*This book was written primarily as a tool to assist parents in teaching their children one of the vital life skills, that of problem-solving. It accomplishes this wonderfully. And it does so much more. Way too many adults don't have that skill set for themselves, never mind teaching it to their kids. This book is just as valuable for parents and nonparents. It's easy to read and offers practical advice. I highly recommend it to anyone wanting to increase their own problem-solving skills or those of their children.*"
—*Thea Singer Spitzer, PhD, principal of Critical Change LLC, and author*

How to Raise a Founder With Heart

How to Raise a Founder With Heart

A Guide for Parents to Develop Your Child's Problem-Solving Abilities

By Jim Marggraff

First paperback edition November 2018

Book cover design by Ela Kaya
Cover image courtesy of Jim Marggraff
Book design by Carolina VonKampen
Photos courtesy of Jim Marggraff

ISBN: 978-1727339574

Published by Jim Marggraff
jimmarggraff.com

To MJ, my wife and life partner who compassionately directed the hour-to-hour raising of our children, about which I now have the privilege of writing.

Contents

Introduction

I've been able to say, "This is one of the greatest days of my life" on more days than I could have ever imagined.

Some of these days are what you would expect—my wedding day, the days my wife told me she was pregnant, the days our children entered the world. These were all incredible days that were extraordinary, though I've had other days get up there, too: The day I watched a 4-year-old girl sparkle with delight as she tapped a word on a page with a prototype LeapPad that my team and I had created and began reading. The day I watched my 3-year-old son dance to the music emerging from a prototype interactive globe when he found and tapped India—he had explored touching countries (though he hardly knew what a country was) and found that tapping the shape that adults call "India" produced music that he loved.

Many, many days walking out of buildings of companies I had founded, I would be totally exhausted, yet exhilarated. I realized that the dreams of each member of my team were being met—we were helping millions of people. There was the day that an employee, Robbie, told me after a meeting that he had thought I was crazy when I held the team to a seemingly insane schedule—and then when we met it, he discovered more about himself and his abilities than at any time in his life and thanked me for this. And the day I signed documents to sell my most recent company, Eyefluence, to Google, making millionaires of a group of young employees I had mentored who I had met just a few years prior and reveled in our ability to bring our technology to the world through Google in a whole new way! These were all days when I realized my dreams could be put into action that truly benefited others.

And it doesn't stop there—watching family members achieve their dreams that helped others was equally powerful. The day that my wife, MJ, earned her first pilot's license at the age of 45 was by far one of the greatest days of my life. Watching her take the steps to accomplish a dream she'd had since she was young—one that would lead her to an eventual career in space exploration research and to become an author—was a powerful experience.

Equally indelible was the day my 18-year-old son, Blake (now 25), called to say that he had won the global Gordon E. Moore Award for the Intel International Science and Engineering Fair for an experimental treatment for cancer, or when he emailed me to say he had closed financing for his second company, Epharmix. Then there's the gratitude I felt as I watched my daughter, Annie, handing out awards to dozens of children on the autism spectrum at her college campus for a running club she had founded. Her club, Bear Cubs at Washington University in St. Louis, enlisted more than 50 college athletes to donate weekly one-on-one time to change the lives of these children and their families. I'd had days where I took my wild ideas into reality and so had my wife, but to see our children do it for themselves? Nothing could compare.

What happened on each of these special days was the result of founding something. On each of these days, someone in my family felt the effect of becoming a *founder*. We each saw something we wanted to accomplish or fix, and we took the steps necessary to make it happen—which is what founders do.

I'm pleased with what I've accomplished over the years with my companies, and I'm proud of my wife for achieving her own career goals. I'm even more delighted that the two of us were able to instill the necessary skills and principles of founding in our two children and that the way we raised our kids gave them the confidence to recognize their potential to solve the problems that mattered to them. In other words, while I love being a founder, I *really* love that we've been able to pass this incredible experience on to our children.

So what does this mean for you? MJ and I would like to share what we did to produce this outcome.

We were intentional about raising *founders*. We weren't aiming to raise *business leaders* necessarily (and we'll get into that in just a bit), but we wanted to raise children who knew how to identify pressing problems and create lasting solutions, and we were deliberate about this from the time they were young to when they were fully grown. We spent many hours discussing how best to parent our son and daughter. What philosophies and values would we instill in them? How could we raise them to be fair-minded and community-oriented? What tools would they need to pursue their dreams and to offer and receive the most from life? How could we instill a sense of gratitude and appreciation for people and events in their life? The approach we took is what I now think of as cultivating a founder's mindset.

And what we did worked. As I write this book, Blake presides over his own digital healthcare company, and Annie has already left a legacy of founding two running clubs for children on the autism spectrum. Our son has always been passionate about health and happiness, and Annie has always cared about giving everyone she meets an equal chance at a quality life—and both have discovered tangible ways to make a positive difference through their passions.

Our children didn't become founders by chance or just because they had us as their parents. It happened because of the intentional choices we made each and every day while raising them, as well as the choices they made through the perspective they developed around the achievability of dreams. These are choices that parents and children can make if they simply know how.

This book is designed to help you recognize and seize the opportunity to make these choices each day with your child—and it's these choices that have the potential to foster a founder's mindset within your young one (and even within you).

Who's a Founder? What's a Founder's Mindset?

When I use the word founder, I'm not necessarily referring to what people often think of as founders: *business leaders.* That is one application of the term, but for our purpose, it's far too limiting.

A founder is anyone who sees a problem, recognizes his or her potential to do something about it, and takes the necessary steps to create a solution. A founder's mindset, then, is a way of consistently approaching the world in this manner.

As we'll discuss in Chapter 6, founding takes many shapes. If you organize a PTA bake sale or host a monthly book club, you're a founder. If you see a major inefficiency at your job and propose and drive an idea that fixes it, you're a founder. As you read this book, I encourage you to think of "founders" as people who bring something new to the world, whether that's a product, idea, event, or piece of art. The bottom line is, founders aspire to create meaningful, strategic solutions that will make some corner of the world, no matter how small, a better place.

My path as a founder has been an entrepreneurial one, and I've started several successful companies that have had a big impact for many people. But starting a business was simply the vehicle through which I believed I could make change. I never thought, "OK, it's time to start another company" for the sake of starting a company. I founded companies so I could bring ideas I believed in to the world, just as Blake is doing. But MJ's and Annie's roads as founders looks different from that. MJ's road led her to write *Finding the Wow: How Dreams Take Flight at Midlife*; from there, her road led to NASA, the International Space Station, and to the University of Southern California for her doctorate to address long-duration space flight. As an author, she's helped many people find meaning and fulfillment. And Annie's path looks different from all of ours.

Bottom line? Your path as a founder doesn't have to be a business. What you found is far less important than the fact that you're founding something to address an issue or follow a passion; it's the thinking and action—not the specific product—that makes you or your child a founder.

Why Raising a Founder Matters

Why would you want to raise a founder, anyway?

Founders are world-changers and difference-makers. A problem-solving framework like the founder's mindset isn't merely a mental model you deploy in moments of crisis. It's a way of approaching and interpreting the world around you. Problem-solving skills empower you to pursue ideas and enact change when you encounter injustices. These skills enable you to hold yourself accountable and become the person you want to be. Most importantly, they help you teach your children to do the same.

Anyone can identify problems (though not everyone can identify the *right* problem, as we'll discuss in Chapter 1). There's no special insight involved when someone says, "Poverty is a tragedy we should solve" or "Cancer is a devastating disease." But founders—the people who lead movements and create lasting impact—don't just observe or react to problems. Founders know how to do something about problems, and they take action.

Teaching children how to problem-solve and think like founders goes a long way in supporting their development into self-actualized human beings. Equipped with the right mental tools, children will explore and innovate throughout their lives. They'll grow bolder with each success, and there's no telling what they'll achieve as their knowledge and confidence expands.

As Blake and Annie grew up, MJ and I wanted to instill in them a sense of gratitude and responsibility. We spoke with them often about how fortunate they were to have been born in the United States, where they enjoyed personal freedoms, lived in a safe home with food on the table each night, benefitted from great healthcare and educational opportunities, and were physically and mentally capable of achieving anything they desired. MJ and I have much to be grateful for as parents, but it was important for our kids to understand their good fortune as well. Malcolm Gladwell writes in his book *Outliers* that good timing played a role in Bill Gates' and Steve Jobs' successes. Yes, they were exceptionally intelligent visionaries. But they also came of age at a time when their skill sets were uniquely suited to the technologies of the era, and they were able to create world-changing companies partly because of this timing. Sometimes people get lucky, and I believe that when they do, they should give thanks by paying it forward.

Although we weren't necessarily trying to raise the next Gates or Jobs, MJ and I felt compelled to raise children who recognized the gifts they had been given through circumstance, in addition to their natural talents, and who contribute to the world in a meaningful way to honor both. I impressed upon them the opportunities inherent in growing up with instant access to the world's information at their fingertips. I told Blake and Annie that you're only limited by your curiosity, your self-discipline, and your willingness to pursue your passions as far as they'll take you.

You'll meet Blake and Annie in the pages of this book, and you'll find that young as they are, both have already made significant impacts on their communities. I share many stories of how MJ and I cultivated a founder's mindset in our children and offer suggestions for how you can do the same. While every child's path is different, I am confident that, through various tips and activities, you will develop the skills you need to spark incredible conversations within your family and will help your children develop problem-solving skills, empathy, and resilience—and become founders as well.

'But I'm Not an Entrepreneur!'

You may not have a background in entrepreneurship—maybe you don't have a background in business at all. That's fine! It won't affect your ability to raise children with a founder's mindset.

I often speak with parents who resist the idea that they can teach their children to be founders. Unless parents consider themselves entrepreneurs, they might not see themselves as founders and may believe they lack the skills and experience to help their kids become leaders. But that simply isn't true. No matter your professional background or economic circumstances, you can develop a founder's mentality and impart that to your children. You can cultivate critical founder attributes, such as gratitude, compassion, empathy, and self-awareness, within yourself and teach your kids through your examples.

I may have been an entrepreneur when I raised our children, but when my parents were raising me, neither of them were leading a business. In fact, our children's upbringing was quite different from my own. I didn't have the ideal environment to develop a founder's mindset, and not just because neither of my parents were particularly business-savvy. My biological father was physically abusive, and violent outbursts darkened my early youth, prompting my parents to divorce when I was 4 years old.

To make matters worse, I had a speech impediment. People could barely understand me. I was small for my age and had a droopy eye, and my mother placed me in a special needs class, where my teachers assumed I wouldn't amount to much. My relatives viewed me as a child who would struggle in life.

Even though I didn't say much, I was always listening; conflict made me anxious, but I learned from it. In many instances, I observed that people were talking (or yelling) past each other. Some seemed to enjoy the confrontation, and I realized they were fighting or arguing for the sake of arguing. They didn't care whether they were right, and they weren't actually looking to solve problems. The exchanges simply provided a platform to proclaim opinions. To this day, I look at a world where many people believe that the ultimate method of addressing conflict is violence. I see a future world where the notion of violence to address conflict will no longer be a part of our thinking.

With training, I overcame my speech impediment and began asking questions. Because I was small and timid, people didn't feel threatened by me. They opened up to me, and eventually I grew confident enough to intervene in arguments. First, I would encourage both parties to empathize with one another. Then I'd ask them to define their own assumptions and concerns. Finally, I'd zero in on a common problem they could both agree to solve—the problem to solve, or PTS, although I wouldn't call it such until many years later.

I learned a great deal during those years from my mother. I knew at a young age that I didn't want to spend my life in contentious, violent relationships. Thankfully, those early experiences helped me not only to manage interpersonal tension, but to also focus on identifying root problems. Because problem-solving is one of the most important skills a leader possesses, I believe my years of adversity made me uniquely suited to entrepreneurship. Furthermore, my mother's mission was clear: She would not allow her children to be limited by anyone, least of all themselves. I believe much of my success in life traces directly back to her and what she taught me about determination and resilience.

Before MJ and I became parents, we talked often about the values we would impart to our children. During those conversations, I recalled how much my mother's early lessons stayed with me and shaped the person I became. No matter how difficult life become, she told my siblings and me, "You can do anything you set your mind to." She repeated this over and over again, and she reinforced the message by encouraging us to read books like *The Power of Positive Thinking* and *Enthusiasm Makes the Difference*.

Knowing the effect parents have on their children's worldview, we've been quite mindful about what we teach Blake and Annie. My mother taught me that I should use my skills and abilities for a purpose, and I wanted our children to have such skills and be able to use them for the purposes of their choice as well. The best way to do that, in my experience, is to become a founder. I hope this book will serve as a starting point for your family's conversations about what it means to be a founder and how you can cultivate the founder's mindset in your home.

That said, raising a founder is demanding. All parents want what's best for their children, and we make countless decisions every day about how best to safeguard their well-being or set them up for success. But too often, parents don't include their children in that process. They're too consumed by what's going on at work or in their other responsibilities to sit down with their kids and explain *why* they make the choices they do and *how* they've come to their conclusions. This lack of communication creates great tension within families, and while it doesn't prevent children from becoming founders, it stacks the odds against it.

To raise a founder, you must be conscious of your choices. You must know how to identify and solve the right problems, a process we'll discuss in depth in Chapters 1 and 2. You must be clear with your values so that you can live with authenticity in front of your children and teach them to do the same. Above all, you must be willing to involve your kids in the tough conversations, and you must share your work and your life with them.

Kids learn so much from their parents, and they pick up on much more than we realize. Inviting your children to paint with you or to write a report or to cook a meal exposes them to all kinds of skills and questions that will spark exciting, teachable moments for you both. Conversations about family conflicts and frustrations are also incredibly instructive, though they are more emotionally challenging. But if you're willing to engage your children more than may seem necessary or appropriate, you'll have the opportunity to shape their values and the lens through which they see the world. At times, they'll be disinterested and question the value or purpose of an exercise or conversation. I encourage you to stay committed to your long-term goal. As parents, we know that children don't always know what is best for them or their future.

Once your family begins thinking like founders, you'll find mini-founding opportunities everywhere, whether you choose to plant a vegetable garden with your kids or organize a neighborhood watch. The act of founding something together will create wonderful opportunities for you to teach your children the skills and attitude they'll need to become well-rounded, impactful, happy, and fulfilled individuals.

Here's what to expect as you read:

Chapter 1: What's the PTS?

We'll start by talking about defining the problem to solve (PTS). In any situation, there are two types of problems: ostensible problems—the ones most people get hung up on—and the right problem to solve. Founders know how to identify that PTS and work toward a solution. In general, better problem identification leads to improved communication, more effective solutions, and more harmonious family dynamics.

Chapter 2: The Founder's Top 3

In this chapter, we'll delve deeper into problem-solving strategies by examining the three questions every founder must ask: why, how, and what. Everything we do hinges on the why—why do we pursue certain careers, befriend certain people, parent according to a particular philosophy? The how and the what dictate the way our whys manifest in our lives.

Chapter 3: How to Think

Now that we've established a strong problem-solving foundation, we'll talk about strategies for thinking like a founder. These strategies include cultivating resilience, resisting defeatist thinking, developing mental patterns, and overcoming challenges to achieve your goals.

Chapter 4: How to Feel

Empathy is a core attribute of founders, which is why I've devoted an entire chapter to it. We'll talk about what it means to teach your children empathy and how having a compassionate worldview will help them become well-rounded, emotionally mature people.

Chapter 5: How to Lead

Leaders are risk-takers, and risk can be tough for parents to swallow. We'll spend some time talking about how to help your children safely pursue their interests and cultivate essential founder qualities, such as confidence, independence, and self-ownership.

Chapter 6: How to Found

Here's where the rubber meets the road. This chapter provides final actionable steps for molding your children into self-motivated founders who meet the world with open hearts and a keen ability for making change. Everything leading up to this chapter comes together here.

Each chapter will contain scientific and psychological background information on the concepts discussed in the chapters along with plenty of stories from Blake's and Annie's childhoods so you can see what raising a founder really looks like. At the end of each chapter, you'll find a section titled "Tools, Fun, & Magic Moments" that will provide you with tips, resources, or other final thoughts to tie the chapter together.

The rewards of raising your children to be founders are many. You will experience moments of immeasurable pride and humility as you watch them transform into thoughtful, capable young adults. But I warn you—kids learn quickly, and before long, they just may turn those tactics back on you, albeit to a hilarious and heartwarming effect.

I hope you find this book and the science, stories, and suggestions within it accessible and helpful as you chart your own journey—and that of your children—to founding what matters most, now and in the future!

Chapter 1
What's the PTS?

Day in and day out, what do founders do?

There are endless potential answers to that question, but they all boil down to one key action: Founders solve problems. It's what they do each and every day, all day. The whole reason founders pursue a project or a business endeavor is to solve a problem, and they address many issues along the way. Solving problems is what makes them independent leaders that others want to follow.

Problem-solving isn't limited to founders, of course—human beings in general are perpetual problem-solvers. We manage conflict all the time, often without realizing it. When you plan an alternate route to avoid traffic so you can arrive at a meeting on time, you're solving a problem. When you negotiate work duties with your spouse so you can stay late at the office to finish a project, you're solving a problem. When you substitute lemon for cream of tartar in the Christmas cookies you're baking with the kids, you're solving a problem (and avoiding the madness of the holiday grocery rush).

For all of this problem-solving experience, however, we don't always tackle our challenges efficiently. That's unfortunate, because good problem-solving skills are essential in every aspect of life—and they're nonnegotiable for founders. Challenges are a constant of the human experience. The better we are at navigating through them, the happier our lives will be.

The biggest stumbling block for most children (and, let's be honest, most adults, too) is that they can't identify the root problem, or the problem to solve (PTS). Identifying the correct problem to solve is the cornerstone of what it means to be a successful founder.

The goal of this chapter is to outline the difference between an everyday problem and a PTS, explain why identifying a "core" problem is such an essential part of the founder's mindset, and give you a starting place for helping your kids identify those problems to solve.

What's Your Problem?

The PTS is different from just any old problem, as the obvious problem you (or your kids) are facing won't always be the problem you *really* need to solve.

Take this, for example: Peter Bregman, a CEO, once shared his aha! problem-solving moment in a Harvard Business Review article titled "Are You Solving the Wrong Problem?"[1] No matter what Peter and his wife tried, they could not stop their three kids from bickering in the morning. Meditation, mediation, rewards, punishments—nothing quelled the tide of insults and complaints.

Then Peter realized he was focusing on the wrong problem. He noted in the article that his coaching experience has taught him this: "If you've tried to solve a problem with every solution you can think of, your challenge isn't finding a better solution. It's finding a better problem."

In Peter's house, the issue wasn't his children's relationships with one another. It was, as he described, a "morning problem"— their energy levels when they woke up. The three kids didn't necessarily enjoy fighting, but they were tired, cranky, and short-tempered, which is a recipe for sibling squabbles if ever there was one. By setting earlier bedtimes and making sure the kids drank a glass of orange juice first thing in the morning, Peter and his wife addressed the underlying cause and all but eliminated those onerous battles.

You might recognize similarities between Peter's situation and conflicts of your own, and that's because problem identification and reframing problems aren't skills that always come naturally. When issues arise, we become emotional—anxious, stressed, angry, sad, or a combination of those feelings. These emotions cloud our judgment, and we tend to focus on everything but the central conflict. Those with a founder's mindset focus on the central problem, as founders can't afford to focus on anything else. That's not to say founders need to be unemotional, but rather that they know how to harness their energy toward a specific goal.

We're all guilty of letting our emotions get in the way of our conflict resolution, but kids especially struggle with this, as they haven't developed the mental tools to conquer this roadblock and effectively reframe problems.

I've seen this firsthand. When Blake was a first-year Boy Scout, he and I went on a hike with his troop. It was a practice hike up Mount Diablo, a 3,849-foot-high local mountain, in preparation for a big camping trip to Yosemite Valley. Blake had never completed a full hike, and certainly not while wearing a backpack bearing 25 percent of his body weight.

About halfway through the hike, he started to get tired. He was talking less and looking down while he walked. As his dad, I could read the signs and I knew he was losing steam. After a while, we were bringing up the rear with only three other father-son pairs, then two, and then it was just us. I told the dads ahead of us to keep going so Blake and I could take a break. To this day, it breaks my heart to remember the silent tears streaming down his face. I can see the droplets running down his small, dusty cheeks as he valiantly took one determined step after another. He didn't want to admit he couldn't make it to the top, but he was struggling.

What could we do? I considered carrying him to the top, but that was out of the question. He'd be mortified. We could walk back down, but there was no cell service to let the other dads know where we were.

Blake was frustrated with himself. He was worried that if he failed to finish this hike, he wouldn't get to participate in the Yosemite Valley trip. Physically, he was in decent shape. He should have been able to get to the top. But his self-doubt, fatigue, and fear of failure were undermining his confidence and conviction to succeed.

It's at this point—the point of seemingly no return—that we need to help our children reframe the problem. In Blake's case, the problem appeared to be the climb's intensity, but I could tell it was something deeper (you know how we parents sense these things). It was his fear of failure. He didn't want to have to give up in front of his troop and in front of me.

Blake needed to reframe his problem that way. If he could release that fear of failure, the situation would seem less dire. He would be able to shift his focus back to the central problem. Once his tears subsided, I gently reminded him that this was a practice hike. He didn't *have* to finish this route; he was just practicing for the next one. When he reframed the hike as practice and training—not the ultimate test of his hiking ability—a weight lifted. The fear and stress dissipated, his energy renewed, and he met his troop at the peak.

Years later, he shared that story at his Eagle Scout ceremony, and then the tears streamed down *my* face because of the effect it had on him. I know that moment continues to influence him in his business and in everything he does.

If we hadn't reframed that problem and Blake had quit the hike thinking he was a failure, he would have lived with that insecurity for who knows how long—maybe years, maybe the rest of his life. Looking at it through another lens and finding the most important problem to solve made all the difference.

Bottom line? When nothing seems to be working, kids aren't at a point of failure; they're probably looking at the wrong problem. You can help them figure out how to find the right one.

A Note on Acronyms

I coined the acronym PTS a few years ago to facilitate faster thinking and better information retention with my professional team. It's not just some crazy idea I came up with—research supports it. Think about numbers, for instance. If I rattled off a phone number to you, could you remember it without writing it down? Maybe, maybe not.

According to neurologist and mathematician Stanislas Dehaene, around 50 percent of Americans can remember a string of seven numbers. However, the average Chinese speaker can quickly memorize a string of nine. What's the difference? It comes down to how long the words are for these numbers—Chinese numbers take less time to say. That makes them easier to remember, even in long strings.[2]

Acronyms are effective for the same reason. If I use "PTS" instead of "problem to solve," I'm using a fraction of the time (about 60 percent) to get my point across. This allows me to increase the density of my communication, keeping my mind more active.

Imagine that we were having a conversation and instead of using the phrase "problem to solve," I spelled out "p-r-o-b-l-e-m t-o s-o-l-v-e" every time. The discussion would slow to a crawl, and you'd probably go crazy from this snail's pace. Saying "problem to solve" allows us to speak more quickly and focus on important details instead of cumbersome pronunciation.

Saying PTS speeds up the interaction further. Making a concept shorter in the language we use to represent it allows us to process the idea quicker in our minds. Because we tend to process words as they sound, a shorter representation of a phrase improves our working memory by allowing us to work with more information faster. That said, the sooner you teach children to identify the problem to solve and get them accustomed to the shorthand, the faster they'll integrate the concept into their vocabulary.

The PTS in Leadership

The ability to define the PTS is an essential life skill because it teaches children to think before they act, helping them develop a plan of action before making moves. Kids who learn this at an early age are wired to evaluate problems instead of jumping to conclusions and misdirected solutions. Knowing how to find the PTS also teaches kids how to get unstuck when they're stumped. This is essential to becoming a leader, and founders undeniably are leaders (we have a whole chapter on that later on).

It's no secret that younger children aren't great problem-solvers. According to Jean Piaget's theory of cognitive development, children between ages 2 to 7 think egocentrically, meaning they think from their own point of view and aren't great at reframing situations from other perspectives.[3] That's why children often end up in arguments about seemingly trivial matters, like siblings fighting over which seat in the car they get. People who can reason through conflict, however, can navigate through tempers and hurt feelings to identify solutions. People want to be around peers who can point to solutions during stressful times.

Kids who *don't* learn effective problem-solving become frustrated easily and are prone to abandoning situations that seem too tough to manage. Worse, they lose confidence in their abilities to push through challenges—and an early loss of confidence can be an incredible blow to a child's development.

The PTS in Interpersonal Relationships

The concept of the PTS seeps into our personal lives, too, as the way people approach problems affects every relationship we have. I'm willing to bet you know someone who is perpetually late. Meetings, coffee dates, dinner parties—it doesn't matter what the occasion, but this person is never on time. She confides that she tries to arrive earlier, but she somehow ends up in the same pattern.

My guess is that this person never learned to identify the PTS. She forgets to account for traffic, last-minute phone calls, or her compulsion to check email before getting out the door. Or there may be a deeper underlying PTS related to a need for control, a fear of compliance, or enjoyment of unnecessary adrenaline. She's developed a range of habits that contribute to her lateness, but she doesn't put the pieces together to see the root of the problem. In contrast, people who do develop PTS skills—especially early in life—exhibit incredible personal mastery. They're self-confident, live by healthy standards, and enjoy fulfilling relationships.

Before writing this book, my family and I chatted about different scenarios in which defining the PTS had helped us in our personal lives. My wife, MJ, recalled how she used it to help a preteen Annie cope with friend issues.

Annie was in fifth grade, right at the age when kids start worrying about who's popular, who's wearing what, and who has a crush on whom. MJ noticed that Annie often talked about a group of "queen bees," popular girls she wanted to be friends with.

MJ asked her whether she wanted to be friends with them because they shared the same interests, but Annie said no. She just wanted to be part of the inner circle. MJ sensed that there was a deeper need and saw an opportunity to develop Annie's character judgment.

The real problem wasn't being friends with those particular girls, MJ decided. It was that Annie was trying to find where she belonged socially. So MJ and Annie worked out a system of four C's for determining whether someone was worth pursuing as a friend:

- Communication: Is she kind when addressing others, or is she snarky?
- Compassion: Is she thoughtful of other people's feelings?
- Contribution: Does she do things for other people, even if it's as simple as holding the door for the next person?
- Character: Is she a good, admirable person?

MJ and Annie decided that if someone met at least two of these criteria, she was a good candidate for being a friend. These were the type of people whose company Annie wanted to keep.

Annie used that framework throughout middle school and high school. Throughout both, she was friends with people in several social groups and comfortable in her own skin (not a bad place for a growing leader to be). Identifying her underlying need for friendship and inclusion helped us solve her problem, and it provided her with metrics she could use throughout her life in making big decisions, such as the people she would choose to spend her time with.

Getting Started With the PTS

Again, reaching the PTS is not always an easy process, as the problem that presents itself is not always the problem that needs to be solved. Parents, don't let your children (or yourself) become frustrated when trying to find the true problem at hand. Coaching your children on how to identify problems just takes a bit of practice.

Here's a good rule of thumb for narrowing down the PTS: You should have more question marks than periods. When you stop asking questions, a conversation's momentum slows, and it becomes easy to get stuck before reaching your final destination—your central problem.

On that note, I like to apply the five W's of journalism to problem identification:

- Who? Who does the problem touch? List specific individuals, groups, or organizations that have been affected.
- What? What is the issue presenting itself? What will change if it's fixed?
- When? When does the problem happen? When does it need to be resolved?
- Where? Where is the issue arising? Is it only in certain places? Or is it more widespread?
- Why? Why do we need to fix this problem? What will happen if we don't? What are the positive outcomes of solving it? This is the most important question, and—when answered—should be asked again, and again, and again, until you reach a point of sheer abstraction.

Memorizing the Five W's

Here's a fun way to ingrain the five W's in your kids' minds: Get them to memorize this excerpt from Rudyard Kipling's "The Elephant's Child":
"I keep six honest serving-men
(They taught me all I knew);
Their names are What and Why and When
And How and Where and Who."[4]
Whenever your kids (or you) struggle to discern the heart of the problem, Kipling's honest serving-men will bring them back on track.

Each of the answers to the questions you ask your child should help you zero in on the core issue. Too often, people fixate on surface-level problems because they're the easiest to identify. They hammer away at the obvious conflict and are dismayed when the issue erupts again a few months later. Progress does not take root unless you distinguish the real problem from the ostensible one.

Let's use allowances as an example of real versus ostensible problems. At some point or another, most kids will ask for an allowance—usually when they're old enough to start worrying about looking cool or wearing the "right" clothes.

A child approaches her parents and says, "I want an allowance." When they ask why, she responds, "Because all my friends have one." Perhaps her parents don't think she's old enough for such responsibility or they simply don't believe in the practice. Her parents tell her no, they won't be giving her an allowance. The child is frustrated, and when she asks why, they say, "We don't think you need one, and that's the end of the discussion." The child becomes sullen or angry and maybe even throws a fit. The parents are annoyed that they have to explain themselves and that their child is acting out. No one wins in these situations.

While the parents are entitled to raise their daughter how they see fit, there is a more positive way of dealing with this conflict. When kids ask for an allowance, it's often because they want something more than the money. Perhaps they want to save up for a smartphone or video game, or they'd like to buy a pair of earrings that their friends have. Maybe they just want to buy a particular snack at school during lunch. Or perhaps they just want bragging rights to their friends that they have an allowance.

The reasons behind the request for an allowance are telling, and they may shed light on an underlying issue. Rather than saying "no" outright, the parents might ask why their daughter wants to be like her friends. If she repeats that they get an allowance, so she should, too, the parents can probe deeper: "Might it be that your friends are able to buy something you'd like to have as well?"

The goal isn't to provide answers, but rather to get her talking about the deeper motivation for the request. Answering with a definitive "no"—the reason for which is often either "There is no further discussion" or "Because we say so" (or any variant thereof)—ends the discussion, and it teaches kids not to ask "Why?" It does nothing but create frustration and animosity, as well as disempower your children. While there are certainly inviolable rules that must exist for the safety and well-being of your children, overusing the royal "no" will teach them to do the same—to avoid looking for solutions when there isn't one immediately in front of them. Furthermore, regarding founding, founders who treat their employees this way do not hold teams for long, and they certainly do not engender respect and trust from their followers (can *you* imagine working for someone who won't give you any reasoning behind their decisions?).

Communicating to your child that you are interested in understanding the core problem (and sometimes there's more than one core problem) provides clarity about your child's day-to-day experience and creates a safer environment for discussion. She may feel insecure if she doesn't have the same clothes as her friends, and she fears being ostracized from the group. Perhaps she's craving independence in the form of her own spending money.

Once you've hit upon that more substantial issue, you're able to differentiate from the ostensible problem ("I want an allowance because my friends have one") and the actual problem ("I want an allowance so I can maintain my social status and avoid loneliness"). Often, identifying the actual problem—the

PTS—puts you and your child on the same team. It's something to solve together, not fight over.

MJ and I encountered the allowance issue with Blake and Annie. We had reservations about giving them spending money, but the four of us found a compromise after working through questions like the ones mentioned above. Instead of an allowance, we gave them each an "allocation." (Notice the value of changing a word to free ourselves from the baggage and connotation of "traditional" words for concepts. More on this in Chapter 3.) Like many other parents have, we created a three-bucket system: personal money, donations, and savings. Blake and Annie received a certain amount and could decide how much to put into each bucket. That seemed like a fair way to meet their desires for independence while maintaining our parenting ideals.

MJ and I found that a strong, consistent, question-based approach to problem-solving encouraged Blake and Annie to come up with creative answers instead of feeling stuck. That's how we've always addressed conflicts and requests in our family. Some issues were harder to solve than others, but the tough ones presented the greatest opportunities for growth.

In 2001, for instance, back when I was working at LeapFrog, Annie was enrolled in Girl Scouts. One day, she approached me in that sweet way little girls have that makes it impossible for their fathers to say no to them.

"Dad, can you help me sell Girl Scout Cookies at your office?" she asked. She wanted to win top prize for most boxes sold, and the LeapFrog office was filled with cookie lovers. But little did she know that her simple request would lead to a major PTS exercise.

"Sure!" I said. "But first, let's take a look at the ingredients."

At my insistence, our family had eliminated partially hydrogenated oils from our diet. Today, partially hydrogenated oils are more commonly known as trans fats, which are now widely recognized by the U.S. Food and Drug Administration as key contributors to heart disease and poor health.[5] The campaign against trans fats hadn't gone mainstream in 2001, but a conversation with a PhD friend from MIT convinced me to look into the potential dangers. My own research indicated that trans fats were, in fact, toxic, and MJ and I purged our house of every can, box, or bag of food containing the harmful substances. I was also "that guy" when we went out for family dinners who asked the server at Outback Steakhouse whether there were trans fats in the Bloomin' Onion. (The answer at the time, sadly, was yes, which was a less-than-popular removal of a favorite appetizer from our diet.)

Blake and Annie used to cringe with embarrassment when I did this, but they didn't fight me on our partially hydrogenated oils ban. I walked them through my logic, drawing out a diagram of the molecular breakdown for Blake, who had a budding interest in chemistry. He even persuaded his sixth-grade classmates that "trans fats are evil." MJ and I received a flurry of panicked phone calls from parents asking why their kids were throwing away bags of potato chips and boxes of pancake batter.

But when it came to Girl Scout Cookies, things got murky. Annie's commitment to our trans fat-free lifestyle was about to be tested, as was our father-daughter relationship. She tolerated the examination of ingredients until I pointed out that partially hydrogenated oils were among the top ingredients on every box of Girl Scout Cookies. (Today, I am pleased to note that most Girl Scout Cookies are trans fat-free.)

"Do you want me to sell my friends cookies that we wouldn't eat ourselves? That we know are poisonous?" I asked, admittedly ramping up the drama.

Suddenly, I wasn't a potential helper in her quest for Girl Scout glory. I was the dad bringing his food politics into a simple childhood tradition. "But Dad, they're *Girl Scout* Cookies!" My campaign against trans fats paled in importance when Girl Scout Cookies were on the line.

"All right, let me think about it," I said.

Annie sighed, knowing that I wouldn't come back to her with a simple "yes" or "no." I'd want to talk about the PTS.

"So," I asked her the next day, "What's the problem in our Girl Scout Cookies situation?"

"I want to sell them, but you won't let me," she said bluntly.

"Hold on, I didn't say you can't sell them," I replied. "I said that *I* wouldn't sell them."

Like most 10-year-olds on a mission, Annie pursued the immediate and most obvious solution.

"OK, how about if I come to LeapFrog and sell them myself?"

It was a logical suggestion. She and Blake were well-known around the office. I nearly agreed. But then I realized I was falling into the trap of focusing on the ostensible problem instead of the actual one.

"What problem are we really solving?" I pressed. "Why do you want to sell these cookies?"

"Because I have to," Annie insisted, getting defensive.

"Why do you have to?"

"Because I was told to."

"Is that really why?" I nudged.

"Well, we're raising money for a trip, and we're all supposed to help by selling cookies, and if I help the most by selling the most cookies, I can get top prize," she explained. "I just want to do what we're supposed to do, and that's sell cookies because we're Girl Scouts and Girl Scouts sell cookies to raise money. Everybody knows that!"

"But Marggraffs don't want to poison people," I said, purposefully extreme.

Annie rolled her eyes. "No, we don't want to poison people," she said.

I scooped her up, tossing her in the air and looking into her eyes. "So what are solving?" I asked again.

Her eyes lit up with thoughtfulness—a wonderful sight in a child of any age. "I want to sell cookies...and I want to help raise money...and I want to win the prize..." She trailed off, pondering her options.

"I think you've defined the problem," I said. "You need to sell cookies, raise money for the trip, and have a shot at the prize—but without selling *these* cookies."

As is so often the case, when a problem is clearly articulated and you've found the PTS, the answer almost always presents itself. That Saturday morning found us rolling out cookie dough with a smorgasbord of mix-ins. I wouldn't help Annie sell Girl Scout Cookies made with partially hydrogenated oils, but I was more than happy to help her sell healthy cookies made with creativity and love.

Annie came to the office with me and proudly told everyone that her cookies were free of partially hydrogenated oils (a term she could barely pronounce at the time). She outsold her troop, and to this day, she attributes part of her love of baking and her interest in marketing to that experience. Working past the ostensible problem frustrated Annie (and sometimes, it even frustrated me), but it led to a much better solution than me refusing to let her sell cookies or compromising our family's values. More importantly, it taught her how to find the right problem and the right solution instead of battling with the wrong problem or giving up.

If you've never practiced defining the PTS with your children—or even on your own—I urge you to try it the next time you and your child face a conflict. This framework will change your family's life. Not only will you be solving the right problems instead of superficial ones, but you will also be teaching your children to do the same on their own. That's a skill that will only benefit them throughout their lives. The more you practice this technique, the easier it will be for both of you.

Share your own victories of finding the PTS with your kids. Many parents don't discuss their work with their kids, but that's a huge missed opportunity. You may have to get creative in the telling of work stories, especially when your children are very young (more on that in the next chapter). But your kids can learn a great deal from hearing about your experiences, particularly when you share a problem you had and how you reframed it to find a solution. Kids love stories about their parents being heroes, and those early lessons will stay with them as they encounter the world on their own—empowering them to find their own PTS in every sticky situation.

Tools, Fun, & Magic Moments

The greatest gift we can give our children is teaching them to think critically from an early age—it's this that leads to great problem-solving. The following games encourage your children to become observant thinkers. Each of these is fun for the whole family, so you get to learn and improve alongside your children.

The Restaurant Game

Purpose: Developing situational awareness

We often take our surroundings for granted, but in order to become top-notch problem-solvers, kids need to know how to pay attention to their environment. The Restaurant Game teaches us to pay closer attention to our environment by actively memorizing details and looking for things other people might miss. (It's also a great way to entertain your kids before the food comes, rather than listening to them complain about being bored.)

The premise is this: Go out to eat with your family—you could visit a fine dining restaurant, a T.G.I. Friday's, or sit on a park bench where you're having a picnic. Once everyone is settled, choose a leader. Have the leader start a 30-second timer and tell everyone to look around, mentally documenting everything they see. When 30 seconds is up, the observers must close their eyes or put their heads down. The leader then asks questions to see who observed the most about the environment.

These questions might include: "What color are the ceiling tiles?" "What color is the dress that the woman behind Mom is wearing?" "How many lights are in the ceiling overhead?" The questions can get as detailed as the leader wants.

After even a few months of playing this game, your kids will begin to automatically take note of their surroundings. They'll become accustomed to assessing their environments and being sensitive to the mood and atmosphere of different places. Before long, they'll be able to identify which architectural or environmental attributes make them like or dislike a space.

From a critical thinking and problem-solving perspective, they'll learn how to take stock of a situation quickly. By noticing even the fine details, they'll be equipped to look beyond surface-level concerns to identify the real problems and create meaningful solutions. Situational awareness also gives rise to new ideas. Leaders see the world differently than other people, so stoking your kids' curiosity and awareness early is a surefire way to set them on that path.

Describe a Stranger
Purpose: Cultivating empathy

Identifying and solving problems requires empathy for other people. You must be able to take in the details—the way people walk, the lines on their faces, the sadness or joy in their smiles—to glean something about who they are and what they need.

I used to sit with my kids in public spaces and have them study the people around us. We'd be in a park or at the mall, and I'd ask them to look at a person walking by and tell me what she was thinking, what she was worried about, and how she felt that day based on her facial expression, clothes, the environment, and other contextual clues. This exercise helped them become attuned to other people instead of focusing solely on themselves.

For instance, we might focus on a woman walking by pushing a child in a stroller. Each of us would look at her face, her hair, her clothing, the gait of her walk, the lines on her brow, what she's carrying, and whatever other details we could catch before she passed us. Then we'd each share what we thought she was like. Was she happy? Stressed? Tired? Did she work for a big company? Was she a stay-at-home mom? Was that her child or was she babysitting?

The marvelous thing about this exercise is that there are no right or wrong answers. After Blake and Annie shared their observations, I would ask why they made the assumptions they did. This is a great way to discover your own biases and to form general ideas about human beings. If you do this enough, you can predict people's actions based on subtle signals you've witnessed time and again.

MJ and I applied similar tactics in teaching Blake and Annie how to interact with guests. Most parents encourage their children to shake hands and look adults in the eye when they greet them, but the lesson never goes deeper than that. Parents want their kids to be polite, but there's no underlying motivation for helping them engage with people who are older than them. That's why many kids simply ignore adults unless they're more or less forced to interact with them.

But when children learn to proactively engage adults, their behavior changes dramatically. We taught our kids to not only shake hands and look people in the eye, but to also think about their needs—what problems can they help other people solve? How can they make people comfortable in our home? What can they do for others?

That habit of thinking about other people's needs proves incredibly powerful when kids grow up and enter the professional world. So much of people's success depends on making a great first impression. If you can read potential investors or business partners within the first 30 seconds of meeting them, you can win them over by directing your interaction to address their underlying needs. We'll dive into this further in Chapter 4.

Remove the Mental Block
Purpose: Eliminating the point of failure

Note: This exercise works best with older children.

OK, you may not want to use the phrase "remove the mental block" with kids. "Exercise" will suffice for them. But whatever you call it, learning to overcome struggles is key to following through on a problem.

Running a business is a lot like hard exercise. Whether you're writing a business plan, outlining an executive summary, or test-driving a product idea, you're pushing your mental and emotional faculties to the limit. More likely than not, you're also running on well less than eight hours of sleep and are fueling your late nights with caffeine. In short, you're pushing yourself to your limit.

You do the same when exercising. Getting to the next level of physical fitness requires serious exertion and a willingness to push through discomfort to achieve something great. If your child seems to get stuck with schoolwork, sports, or other activities, tell him to throw on some sweats and meet you in the yard. Then ask how many pushups he thinks he can do. Whatever the answer—four, 10, 12, 18—tell him you can help him triple that number. It's all about reframing the problem.

Adults look at me dubiously when I try this with them, but kids are usually more optimistic. Fifty-four pushups sound a lot more achievable to a 15-year-old than to a 45-year-old showing the beginning signs of arthritis. But age doesn't matter. In every case, most people can at least double their number with a little practice.

But first, people need to reach the point of failure. Instruct your child to get down and give you however many pushups he predicted he could do. By the time he's finished, he'll probably be tired and convinced he can't do any more. Give him a break, or wait a day, priming him with the possible thrill of blasting through a record he deemed impossible to beat.

At your next session, instead of counting all the pushups one at a time, tell your child to break them into groups—in his mind! If 12 is the target number, ask him to do three sets of four pushups. If he's going for 16, break them into four sets of four. When he starts counting, have him count each group of four rapid pushups as one pushup. This is a mental trick. Certainly he can do four pushups. It just happens that each pushup is a group of four.

Next, teach your child that any failure from exhaustion occurs due to some "weakest link." If you can strengthen the weakest link, you will increase your performance—in anything you do! For pushups, the approach is to shift the stress to different muscles to reduce exhausting the weakest muscles used in every pushup. This means simply shifting your weight, ever so slightly, in a circle. You begin by pushing up mostly with your right arm at first (say, your first four pushups), then shift forward on your toes for another four, then shift your weight to your left arm for four more, then shift back on your toes to get to a total of 16 pushups (counted as four sets of four). Your child will rely on different muscle groups during each set, so he won't hit the point of failure nearly as fast. Coupled with the mental trick of counting to do only four pushups (as groups of four, while shifting his weight around), he will instantly beat his previous personal best. You can also substitute pullups or other exercises for pushups, depending on your child's abilities and preferences.

Before your child knows it, he's hit his goal. Breaking the goal into smaller steps and reframing the problem mentally provides a magical breakthrough that is highly applicable to many marathon challenges in life.

I can't emphasize how important it is to break big goals into achievable chunks and put perfect practice into play. The end goal often seems daunting, but smaller milestones don't look so tough. Repositioning teaches kids to come at problems from different angles and to draw on a range of skills when tackling tough questions.

My kids loved these games, and I'll bet yours will, too. But once you start looking for opportunities to practice problem-solving, you'll find an abundance of them in your everyday life. Simple memory games, reading out loud, and having family discussions about how everyone is feeling are great ways to strengthen skills that are vital to solving problems. Before you know it, even your youngest will be identifying the PTS with ease—and your family will be closer because of it.

Chapter 2
The Founder's Top 3

We learned in the last chapter that the first step toward leadership is problem identification, or knowing how to find the problem to solve (PTS). Now we'll talk about what to do once you've identified it. After all, focusing on the right issue won't get you very far if you don't have a strategy for resolving it.

This is where the Founder's Top Three—the elements most important to developing a founder's mindset—comes into play: the why, the how, and the what. *Why* are you solving this problem? *How* are you going to solve it? *What*, exactly, is the solution? (Interestingly, I find that many would-be founders begin with what, struggle with how, and never get to why.)

Simon Sinek is a British-American author of the 2009 bestseller *Start With Why: How Great Leaders Inspire Everyone to Take Action*. He introduces the Golden Circle model that asks why, how, and what questions, in this order, for businesses and for their products. Approaching founding with why, how, and what questions around your PTS—regardless of what you are founding—is essential to a founder's success.

We'll cover each of the three in more detail, but in short, the why gives a problem purpose, the how provides a method to its solution, and the what becomes the solution itself. The Founder's Top Three should come in that order, too—you can't come up with a great solution before you have a reason for finding it.

Why 'Why'?

While you need all three to make any kind of progress, the why is by far the most important, most difficult, and most frequently disregarded. This is not obvious, and I learned it the hard way.

Shortly after graduating from college, I teamed up with a buddy to start a real estate company. While looking for a house to share, we noticed that people spent a lot of money to list their homes with the National Association of REALTORS®. We thought we could offer a better option: We called it HomeQuest. It was a for-sale-by-owner business that would allow clients to bypass costly agent fees and list their homes more easily independently.

We scheduled a pitch meeting with a group of investors who had experience with real estate and startups. It was a huge opportunity. But as I explained what the company offered and how our system worked, the one question I didn't answer was, "Why does this company exist?" In my rush to dive into the details, I failed to contextualize our business plan.

The presentation fell absolutely flat, and I felt myself blushing as I blathered on, becoming more embarrassed as I realized I was missing any sense of purpose or inspiration in my presentation. If you want people to invest in what you're doing, you must give them a reason to care, and you must be completely clear on *why* what you're doing is critically important to you personally. Only then will people listen to what your solution is and how you're going to implement it.

This HomeQuest experience was a blow, but I took the lessons to heart. In the mid-1990s, I founded another company, Explore Technologies. This time, however, I made sure to focus on my why. I'd heard that a survey from the late 1980s indicated one in seven adult Americans couldn't locate the United States on an unmarked world map, and one in four could not identify the Pacific Ocean![1] "You've got to be kidding!" I thought when I first heard that statistic. I decided to test those findings.

I covered up the names of the countries and oceans on a globe and hit the streets of Boston, where I was living at the time. I walked up to strangers in Faneuil Hall, toting my globe, and asked them to locate different places on the globe's pock-marked surface. To my astonishment and dismay, the survey's results held true; people were at a loss to place common countries.

Geographic illiteracy was a real problem. But would consumers buy a solution for it? I interviewed people on how they felt about not knowing where countries, their own included, fell on a map. Most of them confided that they were *embarrassed*. They read the news and considered themselves well-informed, but they felt incompetent and ashamed about their lack of geographic knowledge. I had found my why. A feeling. An emotion. A need to know something that people felt they *should* know. Further, and most important to me, I believed that as a leading world power, it is incumbent upon us, as citizens of the United States, to know not only know our geography, but to also be aware of governments, relationships, and what were identified as "National Geography Standards and Skills" following the publication of those incredible Gallup surveys.[2]

The why really does make a difference. Whereas HomeQuest became, at best, a learning experience I did not want to revisit, the interactive globes I would go on to create through Explore Technologies were a great success, and it was this company I co-founded that LeapFrog acquired, leading to even bigger opportunities.

The why is the order within chaos. For founders young and old, beginning with why gives a PTS purpose. Whatever you or your children set out to do, always keep the why at the center—it will serve as your North Star when challenges and setbacks arise.

The How and the What

Defining the why makes way for the other two elements of the Founder's Top Three—the how and the what. Once you define the why, you can move on to the how. It's the how that will take you from why to what. The how defines the process for building your product or solution, and it should provide a clear path to your desired result.

Even though it's not front and center, the why is still very much present in the how. I work frequently with engineers, and I push them on their whys. When I ask them why they do something a certain way, they'll often say, "Because that's how it's done" or "That's how the process works." And parents everywhere often lean on this language when it's difficult or time-consuming to explain the why behind a decision—we've all been guilty of dropping a "Because I say so!" when we're being asked something. But in these situations, the person asking wants to know the logic behind a process and how each step leads to the end goal. Why do it this way and not another?

If you get the how right, you should end up with your what—a purpose-driven solution crafted through intention and love. After all that work determining the PTS, the why, and the how, the what should come fairly naturally.

The why is here, too. Every facet of your solution should correspond to the why. In my founding roles, I drill into these questions with my team all the time because I believe it's really important to make those connections. I trust my team members to excel at their jobs and make decisions. I just want to know why they have made the choices they did.

The Founder's Top 3 in Action

Many of the best whys originate in personal experience. There's no greater motivator than experiencing a pain point yourself—in fact, watching my kids learn to read shaped my thinking while developing the LeapFrog LeapPad. By the time we're parents, we've been reading so long that we've forgotten how difficult learning to read actually is. As I witnessed Annie and Blake struggling to connect wiggly shapes on a piece of paper to names and then to sounds, I knew there had to be a better way. I also knew my kids weren't the only ones who would benefit from an updated approach to learning how to sound out words and read.

One of the main fears parents of young children face is that their kids won't learn to read. Parents don't want their sons and daughters to fall behind, nor do they want to seem negligent. The stress is enough to keep you up at night, so I knew parents would appreciate a fun and engaging way to help their kids learn. It was another why to motivate my work.

My team and I devised an interactive book that provided audio feedback when kids touched different letters and words on paper with a stylus. I managed to arrange a meeting with the former CEO of Toys"R"Us to ask whether he thought our product would sell. He said the device was too confusing for parents and too uncool for kids. Video games were all the rage; paper was out, screens were in. I listened carefully to why he said what he said, asking many questions, then incorporated his suggestions to evolve the product concept.

The real test of our concept was whether kids would use the product. During early product tests, I expected the kids to be amazed by the technology. Instead, they were underwhelmed. They would get excited when they used the stylus to touch a letter and hear its sound or touch a frog and hear it say "ribbit." But to my surprise, they stopped after one touch. I thought the kids would be exploring all over the page, but they gave up immediately.

To the adults in the room, the technology seemed magical. But for the kids, there was no reason to engage. Aside from hearing a chuckle from Winnie the Pooh or Tigger, they didn't gain anything from the experience. There was no reason—no *why*—motivating the kids to continue exploring.

The content went through several iterations as we added music, stories, and challenges to keep kids interested. We included autoprompts and guidance, we gave them puzzles to solve, and most importantly, we gave them a sense of mastery and control and appealed to their emotions, understanding how each and every touch would make them feel. Eventually, we hit upon an unprecedented winner. The technological-emotional connection was our how, and the first LeapPad was our what. But at every stage, we were guided by our why. We ended up helping an estimated 100 million kids with their reading skills in six years.

Nurturing Curiosity

Let's take this theory to practice in your own household. Implementing the why, how, and what framework into your children's lives complements their natural curiosity. From the day they're born, children begin making connections about their surroundings and how to get what they want. Before they've uttered their first words, they've identified ways to get their needs met. A hungry baby learns fairly quickly that crying will bring his mother running; the same goes for when he's in pain or a wet diaper is making him uncomfortable. Babies learn these tactics by making observations about the world.

The best thing you can do for your child is to nurture and indulge this curiosity by providing a highly stimulating environment. Children who suffer from a lack of sufficient input develop brain abnormalities.[3, 4] They're also more likely to fall behind in language development. It's absolutely crucial that you talk with your children as much as possible from a young age to establish trust and encourage their linguistic and cognitive development. Your child may be too young to respond to you verbally, but that doesn't mean she's not listening.[5, 6]

Burton L. White's seminal work, *The First Three Years of Life* (which has been updated since its original 1975 publication), strongly advocates for creating highly stimulating childhood environments.[7] MJ and I participated in a parents' group led by White during the first three years of Blake's life. Dr. White walked us through what to expect on a month-by-month basis. He visited our house and observed our interactions with Blake, and his insights played a critical role in how we parented both Blake and Annie. He was a driving force in our decision to incorporate critical thinking and cognitive development activities into every aspect of our kids' environments, and his insights into parenting are reflected in this book and the exercises suggested in it.

Young children have insatiable appetites for information. Their constant asking questions provides limitless opportunities for teaching them how to think. Rather than simply giving them an answer, you can walk them through your logic and expose them to problem-solving approaches. Modeling rational, scientific thinking makes an incredibly powerful impression, and it encourages children to think through problems in a similarly logical way.

To Motivate Anyone to Do Anything, Give Them a Why

Despite my early childhood challenges, I feel fortunate to have always been curious and inventive. I like to ask questions and figure out how things work, and people often come to me with ideas for new projects. Following the Founder's Top Three process allows me to explore a range of concepts and opportunities because I know how to tackle them effectively.

Naturally, I also taught this methodology to our children. Not only did I press them constantly on their own whys, but I also answered any and all questions with gusto. If I didn't know the answer, I would get excited about researching it with them, thereby motivating them to learn. I encourage you to do the same with your young ones; the way you respond to your kids' questions—with excitement and enthusiasm—makes all the difference to their attitudes about learning and problem-solving.

Additionally, talk to your kids. Share highlights and interesting anecdotes from your work and relationships to involve them in your life. As soon as Blake and Annie were old enough to understand what I do, I included them however I could. They were a source of inspiration for me, and I wanted them to be part of my world. Explaining my thought processes and how I worked through problems at the office helped our children form models for how to deal with obstacles in their own experiences.

To be clear, teaching your kids about why, how, and what doesn't need to be boring or pedantic. I never wanted Blake and Annie to think learning was a drag, so MJ and I made educational activities into games. We also tied those concepts to their real-world goals and needs.

For instance, we'd teach the kids SAT vocabulary words during breakfast on weekend mornings. We started this when they were young, so it was normalized and never felt like homework. Then we'd cement the spelling and vocabulary with a game called "Ghost." This game centers around word puzzles; the first person begins with a letter, then, in a cyclical pattern, the other players add more letters to the growing term—without being the player to complete the word. We would all take turns adding letters, transforming it into a new word to avoid giving the last letter. The more vocabulary words you know, the better you do at this game.

As Annie described it, "There was a definite 'why' here. Why should you know those vocabulary words? It's so you can play this game with us and win." We weren't drilling them for their SATs; we were playing a fun family game (which, by the way, we still play).

And versing the kids in why, how, and what not only better prepared them to become leaders, but it also made parenting a lot more enjoyable. When we made decisions, we explained the why, how, and what to Annie and Blake. They didn't always like those decisions, but they understood our reasoning. Then they learned to do the same. If they asked for something or wanted permission to go somewhere, they knew we'd be more receptive if they also laid out the why, how, and what. Those conversations were far more preferable than listening to screaming and tantrums in our hallways (we've all been there), and I'm sure they will be in your home, too.

The Founder's Top 3 as an Antidote to Boredom

Registered psychologist Dr. Vanessa Lapointe has said, "Boredom is the elixir of creativity and passion."[8] In other words, a quiet mind can lead to incredible ideas—an excellent springboard for devising a top three for a particular problem. But what's the bridge between boredom and ideation, and when does boredom go from having potential to wasting opportunity? All throughout our children's upbringing, MJ and I looked for ways to use boredom as a catalyst for great, specific ideas—not as an excuse for an unproductive brain.

Here are some tried-and-true strategies we found for achieving this:

1. Look for problems to solve.

Most parents know the frustration of asking their child what he's thinking about and getting an "I don't know" or "Nothing" in response. Sometimes these answers are deflections. But when they're young, kids aren't always aware that they are thinking. Metacognition (the capacity to reflect on one's own thoughts) is an advanced skill, and you can cultivate it by giving kids a strategy for self-aware thinking.[9]

I've always enjoyed car rides because they provide lots of fodder for conversation about what we're seeing on the road. But there's usually a certain amount of idle time as well. When Blake was 7 years old, we were in the car together and some time had passed since either of us had spoken.

"What are you thinking?" I asked him.

"I don't know," he replied, as most 7-year-olds might.

"I don't know" typically indicates an idle mind. Founders and leaders aren't idle, though—they're mentally active at nearly any given moment. I saw an opportunity here to activate his mind and get him thinking at times when his thoughts might otherwise be wandering aimlessly.

"Blake, you know that wrench in your tool kit?" I asked. "I'd like you to think about what that wrench does, and then imagine another tool that lets you tighten things even better than the wrench."

Suddenly Blake was pondering a problem instead of sitting vacantly in the car. I told him that the next time we are riding together, I would ask him what he is thinking and be eager to discuss his problem.

It was a simple exercise that would lead to sustained, increased mental activity, as well as improved problem-solving, creativity, and innovation. I then asked Blake to think of two more problems he would like to solve. He was to choose one before going to sleep each night and think about it as he fell asleep. The next morning, immediately upon waking, he should think about the problem again to see whether a solution had come to him. I asked him to repeat this habit on any of the three problems until he found a solution. With each solution, he should replace the solved problem with a new problem so that he would always have three problems in his mind. Blake began to discover that when you have an active portfolio of problems in your conscious or subconscious mind, the answers began to appear, almost without effort, when he least expected them to.

This is a way of life for me (and how I've discovered my Founder's Top Three for several of the companies I've founded), and I wanted Blake to get in the same habit of mulling over problems regularly and then sleeping on them, because that's how breakthroughs occur. Answers aren't immediate, nor do they arrive as planned; they come to us at unexpected moments after days and even months of pondering them. You'll see a billboard or a picture in a magazine, read a news article, watch a movie, or have a conversation, and bang! You'll realize that you have a solution to one of your problems.[10] It's up to us to develop a fertile mental environment in which ideas and breakthroughs flourish.

Each night, I'd ask Blake about the problem he was focused on and we'd discuss it from different angles. Of course, each of these conversations began with why, then hit on the founder's other two core elements: Why did he want to solve this problem? How was he going to do it? What would be the finished product? When you work with your kids this way, they are doing all the hard work; you are merely facilitating.

2. Provide the right tools.

Now that you've jump-started the problem-solving thought cycle in your children, you need to provide the right tools. This begins with your own behavior. Kids follow your example, so it's really important that you develop your own problem-solving process. When you want to try a new hobby or learn something new, what are your action steps to make that happen, and what resources do you bring in to help? There's no wrong answer other than "I don't do anything." Maybe you call a friend who does the hobby really well, or you go to the library to find a great book on the subject you want to know more about, or of course, go online. Explain this to your children and invite them to go through it with you. Again, it doesn't have to be anything revolutionary—it just has to be a next step.

As your children get older, you can guide them in developing their own approach. You can also get more nuanced, helping them come up with a system for determining what physical tools they'll need to reach their goals. If they're building a computer, for instance, point them toward resources on what parts they should purchase and what tools they'll need for the assembly. If they're making a complex dessert, direct them to helpful resources on the basics of baking. This way, you're granting your kids necessary independence while giving them the utilities they need to develop and pursue their Founder's Top Three.

Knowing what tools you need is especially critical to the how element of problem-solving. We've all heard people talk about how they're going to lose weight, stop smoking, or stop biting their fingernails. They might know why they want to do those things and what they're trying to achieve, but they may be at a total loss for how to get from point A to point B. It's no surprise when they make little progress.

Kids who understand the value of knowing your tools and your process are more likely to succeed at problem-solving—and to have fun while they're doing it.

3. Always find an answer.

Kids love to ask "Why?" And parents nurture their intellectual growth when they respond to the why rather than being dismissive or saying, "You don't need to know that." By engaging children when they express interest or concern about a topic, you create opportunities for learning.

You can encourage your kids to ask questions by setting the example when they're young. For instance, MJ and I would make observations as we were driving with our kids to get them thinking about their surroundings.

An example of this was observing that the hills in California are brown in summer and green in winter, which is the opposite of the landscape in New England. The rounded hills of northern California also appear to have natural stair-stepped tiers. We'd remark on that and ask, "Why do you think that is?" to get the wheels turning for Blake and Annie. Did it have something to do with local farming practices? Soil slippage? A simple observation could lead to lively conversations.

Don't get me wrong, answering your kids' questions isn't always easy, especially as they get older and their queries become more complex. But you must teach your kids the importance of following through on finding answers, as doing so teaches the follow-through necessary to realizing a why, how, and what for any problem.

If your kids ask a question that stumps you, don't say "I don't know" and leave it at that. There's nothing wrong with not knowing. In fact, admitting that you're not an endless font of knowledge is another great lesson for your kids—they'll see that it's OK to not have all the answers, which will make them feel more comfortable asking questions in unfamiliar situations. However, if their questions are constantly met with "I don't know," followed by silence or dismissal, they'll associate curiosity with annoyance.

MJ and I established a policy that no question from the kids would go unanswered. We may not have been able to provide answers right away, but we would always circle back once we tracked them down. Sometimes this meant doing some research with the kids or calling a friend who knew more about a topic than we did. We tried to expose the kids to different approaches to problem-solving so they'd know there were many ways to get the information they wanted. Today, of course, most answers are a few thumb taps or an "OK Google, what is..." away, so there's little excuse for avoiding these questions!

Blake recalls a time when he asked us how much power windmills produced, and his mom and I weren't sure. We had recently signed up for a subscription service in which you could call a hotline (this was before smartphones) and ask a human to find answers to your questions—basically an analog version of Google. I called the number and found the answer to his question, and Blake says that made an impression on him: "It was pretty eye-opening to think that you, as a child, could ask your parent a question and actually get an answer, even if they didn't know."

That's the connection you want your kids to make—just because parents don't have the answer doesn't mean one doesn't exist.

Sharing Your Work

I mentioned this briefly in Chapter 1, but I'd like to dive deeper into this point here. As parents, we assume that our children are uninterested in our work. Why would they care about the ins and outs of accounting or engineering? Because we're their parents! Everything we do is interesting to young children, and they crave interactions with us. And within our context, discussing your job is the perfect opportunity to showcase the Founder's Top Threes you experience each day in your profession.

You don't need to regale your family members with the minute points of your job over dinner each evening. But do share your passions with them and tell them stories of what you're building or most excited to be working on. Don't give up if their eyes start to glaze over. That just means you haven't hit upon the why yet. Why would your children care about what you do? Find the point of interest, and seize upon it—getting your kids to think through how the Founder's Top Three fits into daily life is worth it. (By the way, this is a great exercise for practicing finding the PTS as a parent. Your why is connecting with and inspiring your children. Now how are you going to do it? And what are you going to talk about with them?)

A common refrain among parents is that their jobs are boring in their kids' eyes. What interest could a 5-year-old have in data entry or sales or custodial work? Well, it depends how you present it. Being a custodian often carries a negative stigma, even if you have a college education. If you're a custodian and want your children to have a positive perception of your work, share the perks with them. Tell them about the weirdest, grossest items you've found and the most bizarre encounters you've had on the job (because if there's one thing kids love, it's gross stuff). Share your purpose and your sense of pride and enthusiasm! This is what any good founder does with a new idea.

Maybe you're an accountant, a job that often gets typecast as dull and uneventful. Fortunately, you know firsthand that accounting can be really exciting. You might not want to break out the spreadsheets with your kindergartner, but you can bet she'll want to hear all about how you solved puzzles and mysteries by putting together different numbers and helping people organize their finances—and, by proxy, their lives. The trick is learning how to talk about your work in a way that engages your child— make it into a story, or relate it to experiences she has had. (You may be able to ingrain a lifelong appreciation for math if you engage her in your work early enough.)

Experience in the accounting field provides rich material for stories about problem-solving as well. One of the most challenging parts of this work is giving clients sound advice and seeing them do the exact opposite.[11] As your kids get a little older, share these frustrations with them. Talk them through your thought process—how do you respond in these situations? How do you not take it personally? What are your strategies for getting clients to do the right thing next time? Accountants also work to tight deadlines, another valuable lesson for kids. You can use your schedule to teach them about time management and procrastination.

The point is, every profession offers something interesting and valuable to kids. Every job solves a problem and encompasses a Founder's Top Three. What is it that you do all day? How do you do it? Most importantly, why do you do it? How does it contribute to your employer's (or your personal) mission?

It's all in how you present it. Administrative assistants learn a little bit about everything because they're responsible for making their offices run. Salespeople play a constant game of persuasion, always trying to beat their personal best. Data entry specialists get to talk to computers all day—how cool is that? Stories like these tell of problems you've encountered, whether they're minor or major. At the very least, you'll encounter interpersonal challenges that you can share with your family. Those often serve as excellent lessons in conflict resolution and cooperative problem-solving.

It's up to you to figure out which aspects of your job appeal to your children, but I assure you, they exist, and it is possible to get your kid excited to hear about your work. I'm positive your kids want to hear about your daily whats, hows, and whys—and hearing about them will get their own Founder's Top Three gears turning.

The Rewards of Raising Kids Who Can Identify the Founder's Top 3

Teaching your kids to find their Founder's Top Three for any problem isn't an easy undertaking, but it's incredibly rewarding. You'll be amazed at the ideas your kids come up with when they're in the habit of asking why and following their interests as far as they'll take them.

When Blake was a senior in high school, he was fascinated by radiation and nuclear power. He learned that in some power plants, radiation would hit metal shielding and produce secondary radiation that was even more toxic. Immediately, the why-how-what wheels began turning. Blake wanted to know why that happened and what the implications were. On the face of it, the secondary radiation seemed like a bad thing. But Blake flipped this around to consider how this phenomenon could be applied usefully, which is a great technique for examining a problem.

"What if this secondary radiation could be turned into a positive?" he asked. He hypothesized that the radiation might be useful for localizing cancer treatments. That's a big question for a high school senior to take on, but Blake felt confident pursuing it because he knew how to solve problems. He didn't have answers yet, but he knew how to find them.

Blake developed a concept to test: Inject inert metal particles, such as tin, into a tumor. Theoretically, the tin particles would increase radiation at the tumor site and therefore increase toxicity to nearby cancer cells. At the time, there was a website that sold a variety of "difficult to come by" materials and tools. Blake had saved some money, and we had an arrangement for him to use my credit card within his budget for online purchases.

I returned home one day to hear a strange clicking coming from our kitchen. As I walked down the hallway toward this unnatural sound, Blake rounded the corner and intercepted me.

"Dad!" he exclaimed, with his customary bubbling enthusiasm about any new experiment. "You've got to see this!" I followed him dubiously into the kitchen. He detected my caution and slowed his pace to chaperone me.

I quickly seized upon three boxes scattered around the kitchen from which the clicking was emitting, each with its own cadence and unique sound. On the nearest box, I saw a nuclear warning sign. I promptly scanned the other boxes and realized they were Geiger counters—tools for measuring radiation levels—strategically placed at varying distances from our kitchen table. My eyes landed upon a semi-shiny, fist-sized chunk of what appeared to be ore in the center of the table.

"Blake," I asked with obviously increasing concern, "is that..." He cut me off before I could utter the word I was dreading hearing—uranium.

"Don't worry, Dad. It's safe. It's only modestly radioactive," he said, with the clicking cacophony belying his statement.

"Oh," I said, controlling my astonishment and concern, being careful to show respect for his (questionable) scientific judgement; in act of benign support, I boldly walked toward the table to pick it up. He jumped in front of me, wearing some sort of protective (lead lined?) gloves, and said, "Well, maybe you should...stay back...just a little bit...."

His next radiation experiments were removed from our house. We already had a high voltage power supply in our garage that I had bought him for previous experiments, and he ordered an old dentist's X-ray tube online to use as a more controllable radiation source. Then he and his friend, Matt, approached their teachers for advice on how to test this idea on living yeast cells (now outside our house).

The organizers of a regional science fair heard about what Blake and Matt were doing and invited them to enter the local contest. The boys were informed of this opportunity the day before the entries were due and decided to pull an all-nighter to write up their experiments. To all of our astonishment, they won first place. That win led to an invitation to a statewide science fair, in which they took second place. Then it was on to the big time: Blake and Matt were invited to participate in the Intel International Science and Engineering Fair (ISEF) and were to be flown to Los Angeles for a week of activities, presentations, and judging. This event propelled high school STEM (science, technology, engineering, and math) students to rock star fame with commensurate treatment—food, fun, festivities, and, of course, the fair.

ISEF is a global competition that brings together 1,500 of the best high school science students in the world, drawing initially from 7 million students' science fair projects in 40 countries. Speakers at the week-long event include Nobel Prize winners, academics, and business leaders. Most of the students at the competition have developed their projects in conjunction with local universities. Then there were Blake and Matt with an experiment that Blake had dreamed up and they had run using $100 worth of equipment. They had employed the scientific method for their experimentation on their own, with inspirational and logistical support from a phenomenally dedicated and brilliant science teacher, Jay Chugh, at a public school in Lafayette. Blake and Matt were just happy to be there.

On the day of the judging, Blake and Matt sat in a huge auditorium with thousands of people at an event that garners worldwide attention. The final winner countdown began, and the previous first-place winner of the California state science fair, who had left Blake and Matt in second place, was announced as the third-place winner of ISEF. With their scant hope of winning now dissolved, Blake and Matt shifted their attention to see which of the other incredible entrants would take the global first-place Gordon E. Moore Award, worth $75,000. The presenter started the first-place announcement stating, "This is the first year we've given a prize to a pair of students." The boys froze. "They are a United States team." Their eyebrows raised and their breathing stopped. "The students are from California." Their faces contorted. "And these two students from Lafayette, California, are Blake Marggraff and Matt Feddersen."

MJ and I were not even there. I had visited a day earlier and spoken with Blake, Matt, and Jay Chugh, observing an extraordinary display of science demonstrations and budding scientists. I had asked Blake about the award ceremony, wondering whether I should stay, and he casually dismissed the offer, though thanked me for offering.

MJ and I each received a phone call from Blake, who was speechless, stunned—and evolved. His sense of self as a humble but dedicated explorer carried an air of realization that his curiosity, explorations, and hard work were bearing fruit. The boys had done the improbable—not the "impossible"—and won the Intel Gordon E. Moore Award, sometimes called the Nobel Prize for high school students, for an idea for a cancer treatment they conceived, implemented, and presented at just 18 years of age.

If ever there was a case to show that curiosity, critical thinking, and a willingness to follow through on a problem are critical life skills, this was it.

I want to note that we recognize our family's unique circumstances here (I don't expect you to set up a chemistry lab in your garage), but we also know that Blake's own curiosity and drive played a much larger role than our provisioning. Again, whatever your home and resources are, all you need to do is point your children in the right direction and relentlessly and fearlessly (though trying at times!) encourage and support them. In a case like this, directing children toward their school's science teachers, dropping them off at the library for more research, and searching online for organizations that can help are all tools in your tool belt. Your job isn't to give your kids everything. It's to encourage them and help them find what they need.

Making Time When There's Little of It

Most parents feel there's not enough time in the day as it is, let alone time to add discussions about finding the PTS or Founder's Top Three or play SAT vocabulary games. But you would be surprised at how many opportunities there are for incorporating these lessons into even the most jam-packed schedule.

The next time you're driving to a soccer tournament or waiting for the bus to take your kids to school in the morning, skip your morning dose of NPR and have them put their phones away. Replace those regular activities with some simple math games, riddles, or word puzzles. Make the activity exciting by putting a time limit on the activity, and make the questions harder the closer you get to the buzzer. This is a great way to stimulate your kids and to enjoy more quality time as a family. Just because you're en route to a game or lesson doesn't mean that time together doesn't count.

Once you look for these opportunities, you'll find many teachable moments—even dining out together. In addition to

The Restaurant Game mentioned in the last chapter, you can bring in some multicultural learning by having the kids spin a globe and choose a country. If you're in a larger city, you might go out to eat at a restaurant that serves that country's or region's cuisine. If you're not (or if you simply love home cooking), look up a recipe the family wants to make from the country or region and whip it up together; as a bonus, you have a great opportunity for problem-solving if your local grocery store doesn't have all the ingredients listed.

Even dessert can be turned into a friendly game. When we'd go to a restaurant, each of us would choose a dessert we wanted. We'd take turns describing the dessert—the subtle flavors, the way it would melt in our mouths, the chocolatey goodness—and then vote. All of us got a kick out of trying to come up with the most creative, appealing descriptions, and everyone won no matter which dessert we ended up ordering. Annie, who recently graduated from college, says those great dessert debates gave her an edge in her argumentation class.

Tools, Fun, & Magic Moments

The books listed below have been invaluable to me as a tool for sparking plenty of whys, whats, and hows. Even books that aren't about problem-solving specifically have served as fuel for finding solutions in a productive, fun way.

I recommend reading each of these books and sharing the most valuable lessons with your children. You can even share how you've applied these lessons to your own life. When your kids are old enough, you might invite them to read passages aloud and then discuss them together.

1. *The Prime Movers: Traits of the Great Wealth Creators* by Edwin A. Locke

This book examines what distinguished the great wealth creators of the 19th and 20th centuries from other leaders, and it strongly influenced my approach to leadership and parenting. Reading this made the value of the "why?" question clear to me. The most significant achievements of the modern world were made by people like John D. Rockefeller, Bill Gates, and Steve Jobs, who were relentless in their pursuits of the right problems. They were also comfortable moving into the how and the what and entrenched themselves in the details of what they were building.

2. *Outliers: The Story of Success* by Malcolm Gladwell

This is a must-read for anyone who hopes to become—or to raise—a high achiever. Gladwell looks beyond people's achievements to examine the contexts in which they were raised and how those contexts influenced their own goals and the solutions they developed to reach them.

3. *Enthusiasm Makes the Difference* by Norman Vincent Peale

Enthusiasm makes you a more pleasant person to be around and can help you think better, problem-solve more effectively, become more confident, and manage stress. Problems don't always easily present themselves, and determining the Founder's Top Three can be even tougher. A little enthusiasm can go a long way in lessening that burden. The book offers vital lessons in developing a psychologically healthy and intellectually motivated child.

4. *How to Win Friends & Influence People* by Dale Carnegie

My mother encouraged me to read this when I was in high school, and I followed suit with Blake and Annie. It's essential reading for empathizing with people and understanding why they do what they do. Everything comes back to why, why, why. Carnegie also has an updated version, *How to Win Friends & Influence People in the Digital Age*, which applies the same principles from the original classic to our current era with today's technology.

5. *How to Read a Person Like a Book* by Gerard I. Nierenberg and Henry H. Calero

This book is all about body language, which is so important to develop familiarity with. Understanding others helps you understand the why driving their behavior. Moreover, it will teach you and your kids how to communicate better based on people's physical cues, as well as give you valuable insights in just about any interaction you can imagine. Whether you want your kids to lead companies or to just be in command of themselves, you'll find this book valuable.

6. *Influencer: The New Science of Leading Change* by Joseph Grenny, Kerry Patterson, et al.

Having a what, how, and why is only a part of what it takes to become influential. The authors of *Influencer* discuss many of the other principles behind influence, as well as how any person can affect others. You'll see a combination of science, theories, and stories of people living out those principles.

I'll end this chapter with some wisdom from my friend Eliot Drake, who encouraged me to remove the word "try" from my vocabulary—particularly in the question, "What problem are we trying to solve?"—and to say, instead, "What problem are we solving?" or better, "What's the PTS?" When your kids identify the right problem and are clear on their why, the path toward how and what becomes clear. Afterward, they don't need to try. They just do—that's the founder's way.

Chapter 3
How to Think

By now, you know the two foundational concepts that define the founder's mindset—great problem identification and the means to follow through on solutions. In the remaining chapters, we'll dive into four how-tos that are essential to developing a founder's mindset. You'll learn how to think, how to feel, and how to lead as a founder does, and then we'll wrap all this together to internalize how to go about founding. First up: how to think. Consider this chapter as an extension of Chapter 1 that goes a few steps further into the mindset needed for solving problems.

We touched a bit before on how people with a founder's mindset think differently than those without. It all boils down to how they work through challenges both large and small. Because founders are often tasked with solving the (seemingly) unsolvable, they need to have sharp-as-a-tack problem-solving skills.

Let me illustrate that a bit more. In the fall of 2008, two events occurred that rocked my life as a founder. The first was that Target picked up the Pulse smartpen, which was made by my company, Livescribe. The Pulse launched in March, and the Target deal helped us hit $17 million in sales that first year. We had the tiger by the proverbial tail, and we were only getting started.

But then the other event happened, and it's one with which you're undoubtedly familiar: The market collapsed. I was in New York City the day Lehman Brothers declared bankruptcy, and I won't soon forget the shock that reverberated through the city. I was working on a round of fundraising for our company, and in an instant, money was in much shorter supply. By the end of 2008, the venture capital firm Sequoia had released its doomsday memorandum advising companies to hunker down, cut spending, and downsize their staffs.[1] My timing in founding and funding Livescribe was suddenly extremely challenged.

Silicon Valley shuddered at the missive, and Livescribe's board members and I took the message to heart. Despite our explosive growth, we painfully decided to cut a third of our 120 employees—just before Christmas. Come January 2009, we were reeling from the layoffs, but the product was still sizzling. Sales at Target were huge, demand was flourishing, and we were planning on expanding to other retailers.

Given the recent upheaval in the market and our painful but necessary layoffs, however, I knew I needed to pay close attention and work closely with my team members. A third of their colleagues were no longer in the office, and no one knew what the future of the economy held. During executive meetings and department briefings, I monitored the tenor of the conversations, observing people's reactions and body language. Leaders must be in tune with their teams at all times, especially when grappling with uncertainty (hang on to that idea for later).

To complicate things, we needed to prepare our annual business plan for board approval. After returning from the Consumer Electronics Show, I was negotiating with retailers who were interested in picking up the Pulse as well. They loved the product, they told me, but they were cutting inventories due to the economic uncertainty and could not predict or commit to orders. We had a winner, yet we were in a quandary as to how to move forward.

Needless to say, this was a challenging time, but it was also thrilling. With so many interesting problems to solve, my brain was constantly turning over new ideas, contingencies, and strategies. The years spent working to find the right problem to solve (PTS) and reframing obstacles were put to good use during those turbulent days. No matter what happened within the company, I was able to address it directly because my team and I knew how to *think* like founders.

Thinking like a founder is a founder's most valuable asset. People who know how to really think are resourceful, motivated, and eager to tackle big challenges. And I'm not just talking about seasoned executives here. Critical thinking lies at the heart of all great success stories, and children who learn this skill are poised for exponential professional opportunities.

When I advised Blake to always have a PTS on deck, I wasn't just trying to save him from boredom. I knew that doing so would energize his mind in a much broader way and that his thinking would evolve to enable him to see the world through different lenses. If you can look at problems from multiple angles, you'll eventually find a suitable (and more than likely innovative) solution—and that's what being a founder is all about.

Overcoming the Impossible and Embracing the Nemesis

We already know that reframing problems is at the heart of the founder's mindset, but let's dive into that in greater detail. The concept of reframing the problem might sound like a problem in and of itself if you don't know where to start, but learned practices like this one often develop after practicing smaller, consistent habits. It's these smaller habits that will teach your children how to reframe problems—and, by proxy, how to think like a founder.

As you might guess, we had many of these thinking habits in my family, one of which was banning certain words from our speech: "can't" and "impossible." These are *nasty* words. And I should know; once upon a time, I heard those words more than most people.

You might recall that I was placed in a special needs classroom during my childhood. Due to my speech impediment, droopy eye, and lack of confidence in speaking to others, my father had deemed me a lost cause. There was plenty I "couldn't" do, plenty that was allegedly "impossible" for me to accomplish. After hearing those ugly words throughout my childhood and seeing how irrelevant and debilitating words like "can't" and "impossible" were to what I was really able to achieve, I learned that there was no reason to keep them in my or my family's vocabulary.

They're just two words to do away with, but cutting them out of your speech makes a big difference. I've even banned these words in my companies; my employees know better than to tell me "I can't do this" or "That's impossible." Remember why I created the PTS acronym? I wanted to speed up my thinking so

I could focus on the really important concepts in my business, and those shorter terms lead to quicker thinking. A similar principle applies here: Much like the almighty "no" we discussed earlier, the moment you define something as impossible, you end the conversation. Eliminating such dead-end terms liberates children to imagine new heights of creativity and achievement.

There's science behind this idea. In the book *Words Can Change Your Brain*, authors Andrew Newberg, MD, and Mark Robert Waldman explain that even a single negative word will spike activity in the brain's fear center, the amygdala—but it's almost a no-brainer when you think about it. If your kids don't have the option of deeming something impossible, they *have* to figure out a solution. It just might take a little more time and creativity.

That said, beware the urge to allow these words to slip out during difficult moments. (If you're a swear jar family, you might even consider adding "can't" and "impossible" to the list of words for which you have to pay if you say). The more your child struggles, the more inclined she'll be to give up or to lash out by using this type of language. That's when you must gently but firmly guide her back on track. What are the obstacles she's seeing? What is the obvious solution, the one that "can't" work? Now that that's off the table, what are some alternatives? You must be empathetic about removing these words from your kids' approach to problem-solving. As long as those words remain in your kids' vocabulary, part of them will feel they have an excuse to give up.

Another habit we've always practiced is what I call "embracing the nemesis," which is to view your biggest challenge as a friend rather than a foe. Cozying up to your least favorite experiences might not sound fun, but it's a worthwhile practice; it takes away the idea that your challenges are roadblocks and forces your brain to look at them from a perspective of possibility.

At my most recent company, Eyefluence, we were trying to come up with another way to control virtual reality using just your eyes. Too many VR headsets require a user to wave her hands or nod her head, which both cause problems and don't consider people with neurological disorders or spinal injuries. And blinking can be a nuisance. So we needed to find a way to interact without long stares and without blinking or winking (both dreadful user-interface methods). But there didn't seem to be any ideas in academic papers or research about controlling interactions just by looking. The literature was either dismissive of eye-controlled interfaces, or it recommended control through blinking or winking and dwelling (which is simply looking at something and waiting for it to acknowledge your resting gaze).

Then I learned about saccades. As you are reading the sentences in this book, your eyes are hopping, then fixated (resting momentarily, for roughly a quarter of a second or so) to every second or third word. You might think that your eyes are moving smoothly, but they are not. In fact, you physically cannot move your eyes smoothly between two fixed points; your eyes always move in a jerky, stop-start motion unless they are following a moving object! An additional fact, little known to most people, is that when your eyes perform a saccade, hopping from one point to the next, which occurs roughly 20 to 40 times a minute, you are effectively blind. This means that as you are looking around, living your life, you are effectively blind, approximately 3 to 4 percent of the time!

Instead of listening to the literature's limited views, I realized I needed to embrace this dastardly saccadic jump. But how? By studying up on everything I could read about saccades, I was becoming more and more frustrated with this nasty biomechanical behavior. I forced myself to flip my frustration to "embrace the nemesis" rather than fight it. I thought, let me embrace this "helpful" saccade as an opportunity rather than an impediment.

I asked myself, "What if I created a new gaze-based interaction language that presented familiar app icons as 'nouns' and a special activation icon as a 'verb,' allowing you to look from the app icon (an airplane for a travel app, for instance) to the activation icon (we used a green circle) to launch a travel app, for instance? And further, what if, when your eyes were moving from the app to the green circle (during which time you are blind), we took advantage of your literal blind spot and stealthily replaced the green circle with a little version of the app icon—so when your eyes fixated on what you expected to be the green circle and you emerged from blindness, the green circle would now be a small version of the airplane you had just been looking at?"

We built this. It not only worked, but it felt as though the system was "reading your mind," as thousands of people told us. We embraced the nemesis and developed a landmark breakthrough in eye interaction! We made the ostensibly "impossible" possible and amazed C-suite executives and interaction researchers around the world.

You can start embracing the nemesis yourself. What's difficult for you? Maybe it's something like a challenging yet recurring task at work, or perhaps it's something like maintaining a consistent workout schedule. Make it an ally. Make it your friend. Dig deeply into the essence of the problem. Think about how and why you're thinking of it as your enemy, and fully embrace the problem, situation, or challenge as your friend and as something you tell yourself is good. Go online and learn how others are dealing with similar problems. Once you have a clear PTS, become excited about solving the problem instead of avoiding it.

Then, impart this strategy to your children. For instance, I was encouraging this during my car ride with Blake when I asked him to keep a problem reservoir—i.e., to have a problem in his head at all times (starting with our wrench problem). When kids are constantly puzzling through a problem and meditating on potential solutions, they're getting up close and personal with things that challenge them instead of fearing and running from those challenges.

Let's take a look at a common occurrence in kids' worlds, one that involves both of these habits. If your kids are school-aged, you've likely heard them gripe about their homework being too hard when they don't understand the concepts or don't know where to begin. Conflicts with friends also lead to conversational dead ends with children. Perhaps you've encouraged your kids to speak their minds on a hot-button issue, audition for the school play, or try out for a sports team, but they fear social backlash or exposure. "I *can't* do that," they might say. "My friends wouldn't understand—they'd laugh at me." "I'm not good at it." The threat of exclusion is powerful for children, making it all the more important to reframe the conversation. Certainly you must be sensitive to your children's abilities and interests, yet you are also their best coach and mentor to help them face the challenges that you judge to be reasonable to help them grow.

My kids used to tell me, "Dad, you just don't understand." Maybe you've heard this line a time or two as well. They thought I didn't understand what their teachers were asking of them or what they were going through with friends. To be fair, they were sometimes right. I didn't always know the answers to the exact problem my kids were solving. But I did know how to think, and that allowed me to support them anyway. For instance, in helping with math, while I could not recreate the exact manner Annie's teacher wanted her to solve a problem, I was able to guide her through example solutions from her notes or textbook, help her pinpoint exactly the areas she did not understand,

and allow her to discover the essence of the problem that was blocking her. The biggest challenge was not the math, but rather her attitude and mounting frustration toward approaching a problem that seemed unsolvable or unworthwhile. The most important discussions we had were those that helped her overcome the negative energy that was preventing her from thinking clearly, exhausting her, reinforcing her frustration, and blocking her ability to embrace the challenge by looking for a solution. This metacognition, or self-awareness of thought, takes time to develop but is critical for success in many areas of life— including founding.

The next time your child struggles with a homework assignment and insists you don't understand, don't argue the point. Invite him to set the assignment aside and take some deep breaths to calm down. You can't reason with him if he's in a strong emotional state. Empathize with him and validate his *feelings*, but do not reinforce his negative energy. Then talk about the issue he's having. Ask, "What is your teacher looking for?" The ostensible problem is finding the correct answer to a geometry equation or a question on a literature assignment, but you know there's more to it than that.

In addition to wanting the homework turned in, most teachers want to know that their students can think through a problem and grasp the concepts presented in class. Guiding your child to embrace returning to the explanations in the book or his notes is a huge step in empowering him to own the ability to solve any PTS. If the material in his book or notes do not make sense to him (or to you), then work with your child to go online to understand the issue or call a friend who's great with the subject.

If your son or daughter is still struggling with these solutions, suggest a meeting where you can discuss alternative approaches with his or her teacher. This is usually a last resort, as most children will resist this with fervor—another PTS for *you* to help them embrace this nemesis. Include your child so he can witness the negotiation process. Being part of the conversation will make him feel empowered, but it will also allow him to see dialogue in action. When he hits a roadblock in the future, he'll remember that there's room for discussion and alternative paths to success.

Depending on your child's age, you might encourage him to initiate those conversations with his teacher on his own. Kids often believe that teachers either don't want to hear what they have to say or that they don't want to answer questions about assignments, but that's generally untrue—most teachers appreciate a student's genuine effort to have a productive conversation. Teachers don't want to hear "I can't do it," because that's not a productive conversation. But they're almost always willing to hear, "Here are my ideas" or "I'm having trouble here, can you help me?" Perhaps even help your child come up with a script he can rehearse so he feels less nervous in approaching his instructors. Here's an example of how this might go:

Child: "Hi, [teacher's name], can I meet with you before class today? I have an idea I'm really excited about, and I'd like to share it with you."

Teacher: "Sure. Why don't you come to the classroom right after lunch?"

During the meeting, your kid might say: "I have an idea about how I'd like to approach the paper you assigned us. It's a little different from what you outlined, and I'm not sure how to tie it into the assignment. Can you help me figure out how to pull it altogether?"

Teachers are thrilled when they see students taking this kind of initiative. They witness kids throwing up their hands in despair all the time, getting down on themselves, blaming the teachers for their difficulties, or simply giving up. Nothing is more rewarding than students who engage with the materials and get excited about what they're learning, so most teachers will be delighted to be part of the solution instead of the object of a student's scorn.

Kids often forget that teachers are human. Authority figures loom larger than life in their eyes, but as a parent you know that adults—and teachers—have blind spots and shortcomings, too. Letting your kids in on this secret will help them see their teachers as people and relate to them more easily.

When Blake was in high school, he joined the school newspaper, which was overseen by a teacher who we'll call Mr. P. This teacher was notoriously tough, and Blake was taken aback by how aggressively Mr. P challenged his students. For the first two weeks of this class, Blake came home in tears, not knowing how he was going to deal with that environment for an entire semester. MJ and I encouraged Blake to lean in—a term that has become a buzzword in the business world but is useful nonetheless. Rather than see himself as a victim of Mr. P's teaching style, we suggested that Blake try to understand his methods. Blake watched how Mr. P interacted with students, assigned projects, and organized the class. An air of disorganization permeated Mr. P's teaching processes.

Perhaps you've encountered something similar in your own kids' experiences where you just know they're not getting an honest chance at success. It's hard! And as a parent, it was difficult not to intervene on Blake's behalf. Together, however, we brainstormed a way for him to help his teacher on his own. Blake began approaching Mr. P after class to talk about assignments, forging a bond and opening a pathway toward offering feedback. Thinking through a productive solution to his problem wound up not benefitting just Blake, but also his entire class—and it probably helped keep Mr. P from feeling overwhelmed, too.

Had Blake merely accepted his teacher's intimidating methods, he would have been miserable all semester, and he would have reinforced a sense of learned helplessness, which is the antithesis of a founder's outlook. Instead, Blake embraced his nemesis (his nemesis being the teaching methods—not Mr. P himself) and wholeheartedly looked for a way to improve the situation and created better outcomes for himself and his classmates. Blake's story goes to show that eliminating "can't" and "impossible" teaches kids that they are not victims. And that's really important, because founders don't have victim complexes. Leaders field problems and setbacks all the time, and they'd never get anywhere if they took everything personally or succumbed to negative energy. Kids who grow up feeling empowered see the world as being filled with opportunity, rather than a minefield of detractors out to get them.

Thinking to the Far-Off Future

So far, we've discussed critical thinking in a short-term context: "How can we identify this PTS? How can we find a specific solution?" But thinking for the short term only gets you so far. To truly have a founder's mindset, you and your children must be thinking with the long term in mind. Long-term critical thinking is an invaluable skill for everyone (not just founders), but it's an essential piece of using your brain like a founder. Think about it—no founder wants his or her project to fail, so thinking to the future is crucial.

One exercise my family (myself included) has relied on for developing this skill is what we call a Rocking Chair Retrospective (RCR). In short, a RCR helps people visualize their future self in order to understand future goals and realize what steps it will take to get there.

For older kids, maybe 10 and up, have them close their eyes and picture a much older version of themselves—perhaps at 80, 100, or even 120! They're sitting in a rocking chair, looking back on all the decisions and experiences that have led to this moment. Now, have your kids answer these three questions: 1) "What am I most proud of?" 2) "What did I most enjoy?" and 3) "How did I most contribute in my life?" Ask them to write their answers to these three questions on not more than two pages, and be sure they write them in present tense, looking back over their life from that future vantage point, rocking in their rocking chair.

The RCR is an extraordinary tool for parents, older children, and all of us to look backward from the future at a life that hasn't happened yet, retrospectively prioritize what "was" important, and reflect upon why it was important to you. For younger kids, instead of asking them to imagine themselves that far along in their lives (something they likely will have trouble fathoming), ask them how they'll feel about one choice or another in a week, day, or even in an hour, and then discuss why this is important.

The RCR helps a person get out of the present moment and look beyond our current worries and constraints. When thinking about big-picture direction, we need to see the big picture. But it can be difficult to do that if we're fixated on the short-term consequences of our actions. Ask your child (and yourself): What's more important, watching some Netflix now or working on that big science project (or college application or job portfolio) you're hoping to do really well on? And why? The choice seems obvious on paper, but it's very difficult to focus on the long-term from hour to hour and day to day.

Writing an Honest RCR

I recently spoke to 150 MBA students at a Columbia Business School Silicon Valley event. I asked them whether any had written their Rocking Chair Retrospective. The term had no meaning to them. I explained what a RCR was, and they became fully engaged. I then offered to review anyone's RCR if they were willing to share it. I did so cautiously, as I knew that reviewing 50 to 100 two-page documents would mean a significant commitment of my time.

How many RCRs do you think I received from the group?

I received a single RCR. It was most fascinating and shed light on, perhaps, why I received only the one.

The email arrived the morning two days following my presentation. I opened it immediately, recalling the individual with whom I had spoken at the event. Her retrospective comments did not reflect the spark and drive I had seen in this young woman two nights earlier. That same afternoon, I received a second email from her. It began with "I lied"; she explained that she had reflected on her first email and realized that those were not her real answers. She had been afraid to write what she actually wanted her life to be out of fear that she may not achieve it.

So if you do have the courage to write your RCR, be certain to reach for you dreams—and make sure your kids do the same. It is not achieving the specific goals that is most important; it's about asking yourself *why* the achievements in the life you are writing about are important. Your RCR is much more about finding, reflecting upon, and understanding your "why" in life, and it can motivate some extraordinary personal growth and development.

Tools, Fun, & Magic Moments

Easier said than done? Not necessarily—teaching kids to think like founders is a lot of fun, for them and for you. Again, whether or not you're an entrepreneur yourself doesn't matter; anyone can adopt these practices and start thinking differently. In addition to changing up your vocabulary and leaning into conflict, here are some fun and engaging strategies that will teach your kids how to think and spark interesting conversations within your family:

1. Look for teachable moments wherever you go.

We talked about this before, and it applies here as well: If your children express an interest in a topic, no matter how mundane, embrace their curiosity with gusto. Share your enthusiasm, though be sure to let your children lead their own interests so they develop the confidence of coming up with an area of interest and pursuing it on their own. You can further stoke their cognitive fires through intellectually stimulating activities, such as visiting museums or attending cultural events in your area. Make museums a regular part of your family's leisure time, beginning when your kids are in preschool. There are lots of free museums, and many are free for younger kids. Even if they don't grasp every exhibit, your kids will be exposed to facts about different periods in history, various art forms, and animals they never even knew existed.

A museum trip can spark hours, even days, of lively conversations and questions, and you can extend these discussions by helping your kids search for more information on the internet. Doing so provides a nice segue into teaching them how to judge which online resources are trustworthy and which publish false information. Given how much children will be using the web in their school assignments in the years to come, knowing how to separate the digital wheat from the chaff is going to be an increasingly important skill.

Even entertainment-based activities provide opportunities for learning. Our family didn't watch much TV when the kids were growing up, and we only went to the movies occasionally. But when we did take Annie and Blake to the movie theater, we liked to make it an active experience. After the movie, we would take time together to recount details about the plot, theme, character, and setting, as well as what we liked and disliked overall about the film. I've always thought it's a missed opportunity to walk out of the theater, say "That was a good movie," and never give it another thought.

Our kids learned to contemplate what they had seen, and that skill transferred into their schoolwork as well. Annie says that our "movie reports" helped her write better book reports in middle school because she was already accustomed to reflecting on and dissecting plots. What you teach your children at home intersects with every other area of their lives, so make those moments count.

2. Create new language.

By now you know that you need to ban "can't" and "impossible" from your family's vocabulary. Next comes the fun part—creating new words to replace them! When we use the same language as everyone else to solve problems, we often end up circling the same uninspired solutions. Coming up with acronyms, such as PTS for problem to solve, invigorates and accelerates the conversation. Unique phrasing allows our brain to short-circuit bland or outdated ideas to think more innovatively.

If you're uncertain about how to get started, make a list of common terms your family uses. Then ask your kids to think of acronyms for these to get them in the habit of creating unique phrases. To avoid your acronyms becoming stale, expand your children's vocabulary through word games and books. MJ and I often referred to the book *Vocabulary Cartoons: SAT Word Power* when teaching Blake and Annie new terms. The book uses mnemonic pictures to help kids recall tough words and their meanings. For instance, the word "truculent" would be broken down into "truc(k)," "you," and "lent," followed by a sentence-length story incorporating the parts of the word into a silly but memorable scenario; there were also comical images to reinforce the memory hacks in the book. For "truculent," it was a picture of a driver standing aside a smoking, wrecked *truck you* had apparently *lent* to him. The kids loved both the cartoons and our weekend breakfast "fun sessions" introducing them to a new week's worth of words. The approach also helped introduce them to the power and form of key mnemonic techniques—tools for remembering—and got them used to taking words apart and having fun with them.

As you introduce new words, incorporate them into other activities as well, like the storytelling game (which you might be familiar with already). Have someone start off a story with a single paragraph or sentence, and then go around to each family member and have them add to the narrative. Be as goofy as you want with these. In fact, the more outlandish the story, the more opportunities you and your kids will find for using the new vocabulary words. Don't be surprised if these words make their way into everyday conversations in your household and eventually become part of your problem-solving acronyms.

Finally, another way to have fun with this concept is to read lyrically interesting books, such as those of Shel Silverstein, Dr. Seuss, and other playful wordsmiths, out loud with your kids. When you read, read with extreme passion, inflection, and different voices, and have fun doing so! This energy and enthusiasm is contagious, and though you may not immediately see it, it will surface at school in instances you will eventually hear about from your kids' teachers and their friends' parents. This energetic, unabated enthusiasm is a critical founder skill (more on that in Chapter 6). Stories and poems like these are charming, funny, and evocative, and they often include lots of wordplay. Your kids will enjoy the entertaining nature of these books while stretching their minds as well.

3. Revel in novelty.

As a parent, you profoundly impact your children, often in ways you won't realize until years later. Someday years down the road, your kids may recount what was a life-changing moment for them, and you may not even remember it. That's why it's important to take advantage of every opportunity for spontaneous learning and creativity.

One way to do this is to revel in novelty. The instant that you or your child experience a "Wow!" or "Aha!" moment after learning something new that inspires or excites, take that enthusiasm and run with it. Help yourselves think through all the different ways this exciting concept can be applied to other (seemingly unrelated) areas. Look for ways to link varied interests as well. In the example of Annie wanting to sell Girl Scout Cookies that didn't conflict with our family's values, she was able to combine her enjoyment of Girl Scouts with her love of baking to find a great solution. Help your kids connect the threads in their own lives by looking for areas of overlap in their favorite activities.

Practicing this habit teaches kids to make cross-domain connections that lead to creativity and cognitive breakthroughs. Blake once had to make a video for a class in which he needed to present a new product idea. He developed the concept for a "power pillow," which helped people sleep better by using a small packet of sweet-smelling herbs tucked inside it. This was just a class assignment, but you can see how cross-domain thinking can lead to innovative products in the business world as well.

Even as your children are growing up, find times to ask them about moments they remember earlier in life. It will surprise you to learn which events and experiences they recall; this will teach you the type of things that stand out for them. Be sure to look for moments yourself, as well, when you learn of something that amazes you, then reflect on what it is that you are amazed at and share the discovery with your children. If you can distill the higher-level concept that allowed you to see something in a way you had not seen it before, you may be able to apply that principle to other problems. The best moment to attempt this application is when the concept is fresh and new.

4. Practice mental math.

Most kids are able to learn their multiplication tables with some practice and discipline, particularly if they're only asked to rattle them off in order. Once the numbers get bigger or the order gets switched around, however, it becomes clear that what they've learned is closer to rote memorization than any real mathematical principles or models.

Mental math games challenge kids to practice their skills and strengthen their abstract thinking abilities (more on that in the next tip). Rhythmic math, in particular, cultivates agility and speed in kids' thinking. Here's how it works: Give your kids a multiplication question with one single-digit number and one double-digit number, such as 9 x 16, which equals 144. Most kids will try to mentally calculate the problem the same way they would on paper, which doesn't work well, especially as you get into higher numbers. The way we do math in our heads differs from what we do on paper.

Rhythmic math begins with a basic mental math principle, which is to multiply the most significant digits (larger numbers—or, in our example here, the tens place) first, then hold the result in your head while you multiply the smaller numbers (ones place), then add the result in your head. So 9 x 16 becomes 90 + 54, which equals 144.

The next step, which is what makes this approach "rhythmic," is to perform these three calculations to a rhythm to help kids think faster, which means that they will not forget the intermediate products (90 and 54) to be added.

I would begin by announcing the problem, then clapping once for each mental calculation, then asking Blake to announce, to my rhythmic claps, the three values: 90, 54, and 144. This forces focus, reduces mind wandering, and by clapping quickly enough, takes advantage of short-term memory to hold the numbers in your mind to allow "working memory" to kick in—which is when you process items in your short-term memory.

In practice, I would speak and clap the problem, then continue clapping at the same rhythm for Blake to solve the problem. So for 7 x 49, we would clap and speak as follows:

Time	Me	Blake
1 second	Clap	Say "7"
2 seconds	Clap	Say "times 49"
3 seconds		Say "280" (thinking 7 x 40)
4 seconds		Say "63" (thinking 7 x 9)
5 seconds		Say "343" (thinking 280 + 63)

We would repeat this with nonstop clapping up to 10 times in a row, with a new product of a one-digit number multiplied by a two-digit number, maintaining a continuous cadence. We started with slightly slower timing, perhaps two-second intervals, then moved progressively faster.

One other subtle trick is to speak the numbers as concisely as possible to allow for faster speed. For instance, when speaking "280," say "two eighty" rather than saying "two hundred and eighty." Similarly, for "343," say "three forty-three" rather than "three hundred and forty-three." At first, kids can practice speaking the words aloud, then eventually, you'll just clap, faster and faster, as they silently speak and think the words and just pop out the answer.

I practiced this with both Blake and Annie, and today they are extremely adept at mental math, which is an extraordinarily valuable skill for a founder in many circumstances (negotiations, team problem-solving, board discussions, and more).

Another more commonly used approach for mental math is simple rounding before completing a problem. For instance, in multiplying 9 x 16, one can round nine up to 10, easily multiply to get 160, then subtract one 16 (reversing the impact of rounding up), to also end up with 144. As your kids become more adept at mental math, they will become more confident with more advanced thinking and tools.

An associate of mine, Mike Milken, who was a great advocate of the LeapPad, promotes mental math skills as an effective means of sharpening one's thinking. For some great additional tips and support, Google "Mike's Math Club."

Tricks and Tips to Make Math Easier

From my time at LeapFrog, I learned a lot about the common mistakes kids make in developing various math skills. For learning multiplication tables, there are tricks on websites like Multiplication.com that help kids quickly master most of the table, but there are a handful of products (pairs of numbers to be multiplied) that vex many young students. These are 6 x 7, 6 x 8, and 7 x 8, though there are even tricks for these. The discussion regarding rhythmic math is dependent upon fluent, fast knowledge of one's multiplication tables and mental math for addition, for which there are also many tricks online.

5. Extract abstractions from the everyday.

Abstract thinking is being able to hold different ideas in your mind and synthesize them quickly. Your brain processes the information and then comes up with new ways of thinking about what you've learned. Children often learn this when they're asked to write an essay in school—they read or hear a concept and must then distill the core idea into a sentence or paragraph.

Extracting abstractions is absolutely critical for a founder. You must be able to take in information, identify the most important components, and then make decisions based on that data. In fact, that's how any successful organization begins.

Annie launched the Bear Cubs Running Team after meeting a young girl named Jane, who was the sister of one of Annie's high school track teammates. Jane loved to run but was unable to participate in her school's athletic program because she is on the autism spectrum and her condition precluded her from joining a sports team. Upon hearing this, Annie began thinking about other kids who didn't have a chance to experience the joys of team running. Inspired to create a solution for them, Annie founded Bear Cubs, a free program that enables kids on the autism spectrum to exercise and have fun alongside their peers. Had Annie focused solely on Jane's experience, she might have found a solution for Jane's problem, but not for other kids like her. Instead, Annie abstracted the larger problem—the issue of autism within a family unit—and positively extended her thinking to focus on the impact she could have on an entire family when helping autistic children and their siblings.

Frans Johansson describes this as the "Medici effect" in his book of the same name.[2] The greatest advances occur, he argues, when people from different disciplines collaborate or when thinkers expand the scope of their pondering outside their areas of expertise—when they're distilling their field's core aspects into abstractions and seeing how they relate to other fields. Biomimicry—where architects and engineers come together with biologists and ecologists to create structures and processes that mimic nature—is one current example. In 2012, for example, Zimbabwe's Eastgate Centre solved an air conditioning crisis by erecting skyscrapers that mirror termite mounds.[3]

Children who grow up to be interdisciplinary students and develop the skill of extracting abstractions from details will make connections that others cannot see and build companies their peers have never even dreamed of.

When you can synthesize what you see, hear, and feel into a mental model, you spark new ideas and design creative strategies to previously unsolved problems. It's one of the most powerful life skills a person can have, and here's the good news: Each one of the tips I've just mentioned helps kids develop this ability to synthesize. Children who are always asking why—always exploring their ideas and seeking out new ways to engage with their surroundings, always focusing on the PTS, eliminating negative energy to develop a positive attitude toward problem-solving, and embracing their nemeses—are kids who grow up to change the world.

Here's what it looks like when all of these attributes come together:

"Nice to meet you, Blake," said my friend Richard, whom I had just introduced to my 16-year-old son (this was a few years ago). "Your dad tells me you're interested in using chemistry to save lives. I'm the head of UC Berkeley's Molecular Cell Biology department, and we've just had a breakthrough in understanding how our bodies copy DNA, which we hope will lead to more effective cancer treatments."

Now, if Blake had been like most teens—or even like many adults—he might have offered Richard a quick hello before quickly exiting the conversation. Instead, he told Richard it was a pleasure to meet him and asked whether Berkeley's gene expression studies might impact cancerous cell responses in radiation therapy, one of Blake's key areas of interest, as you might remember from earlier in the book.

It was a remarkably mature way of responding, but it didn't happen by accident. Blake demonstrated the full range of thinking skills he had developed in his adolescence:

- He activated his natural curiosity to listen to what Richard was saying.
- He drew on a problem he had been mulling in the back of his mind—enhanced radiation cancer treatments—to connect it to the present conversation.
- He ignored his doubts about the viability of his idea, which otherwise would have prevented him from speaking up.
- He asked a question at the intersection of his knowledge and the work of Richard's Berkeley colleagues.
- He reveled in the novelty of learning about the molecular cell biology team's research.

Could Blake have responded in this manner (even without the detailed knowledge) when he was a younger child? Probably not—I wouldn't suggest insisting that your 4-year-old do this next time he meets a houseguest. In Blake's case, he had spent years pursuing his interests and ideas at that point, not to mention honing his listening skills. But these are the types of interactions kids are capable of as they develop their thinking skills.

Chapter 4
How to Feel

"Julie, can you touch a word?" I asked the 4-year-old girl sitting beside me. My team and I were testing a LeapPad prototype, and I was expecting a big reaction from our young tester. Instead, she looked at me quizzically, holding the stylus we had given her in midair.

I was puzzled. I thought, "Is she just shy? Shall I repeat my request?" Then it struck me. She didn't know what the word "word" meant.

"Touch here," I said, pointing at the word "it," which was printed on a piece of paper taped to a Wacom digitizing tablet. Julie hesitantly tapped the stylus to the word, but froze when she heard the word "it" emanate from the computer's speaker. I encouraged her to tap the next word, "wiggles," and it sounded from the speaker. She continued. We heard, "'It wiggles, Leap! The top one, here. My tooth, it's loose,' cried Lil. 'Oh dear.'" A chill ran down my spine after three years of work to reach this moment. Julie was starting to read—at least, she understood that the little black squiggles on the page formed letters that made sounds, which blended together to make words that produced a sentence, which communicated an idea, or, in this case, a story.

The delight on Julie's face when she first made that connection told me I was onto something. From 1995 to 1998, my team and I had been developing the concept of paper-based multimedia as a mechanism for teaching kids to read. The idea came to me at 4 a.m. one morning when MJ and I were living in Concord, Massachusetts. Blake was only 3 years old at the time, and I had been pondering how I could help him learn to read; plenty of what we discussed in Chapters 1, 2, and 3 led me to come up with the idea for the LeapPad.

After our initial tests, the LeapPad team and I brought our prototype to the top retailers in the country to show them the magic of this educational "toy." Their response was not positive. "This is a really cool demo," we heard over and over. "But kids don't want paper. They want video games. They want screens. Parents will never buy it. They won't understand its value when they see it on a store shelf. It won't sell."

Six years, 100 million literate children, and $1 billion in sales later, we proved the naysayers wrong. The LeapPad ended up in more than 77 percent of households in the United States with kids between the ages of four and seven from 1999 to 2005. It ranked as the No. 1 toy in the United States, United Kingdom, and Australia for many years running, and we've heard from young adults who say the LeapPad helped develop their reading and learning abilities.

How did we do it? By empathizing with our target audience members and understanding their educational, emotional, and social needs, and, critically, the needs of their parents—those who would be our actual customers.

At each stage of the LeapPad's development, I asked our producers, writers, artists, and sound designers the same questions: Why...? How...? and What...? "Why are you designing your game (or question, art, or music) as you are? How can you improve children's engagement, their awareness of growth, and their curiosity? What problem are you solving?" You already know that asking those questions is essential to founding a project with substance. But equally importantly, I asked them, "How will this make children *feel*? How will this cause them to interact with their family and friends? What will make them aware of their abilities and their growth? What will give them a sense of mastery and control? How will this impact their relationship with their parents?" Every aspect of product development—from the game icons to the audio cues to the musical interstitials and background music to how hard Winnie the Pooh laughed when his tummy was tickled with the stylus— centered around these questions. No detail was insignificant; each step of the user experience was designed to inspire wonder and a sense of achievement, mastery, and control.

As I mentioned in Chapter 2, LeapPad was borne of an important why. Why was this product relevant? Why did people care about it? Why would kids and parents need it? I knew from experience the anxiety parents feel about whether, and when, their kids will learn to read. I also witnessed my own kids' frustrations when first learning this all-important skill. The goal was to create a product that would make learning to read fun and attainable for all children, give parents a tool for helping their children succeed, and demonstrate their success—and above all, to raise literacy rates in the United States and around the world.

This merging of purpose and product is empathy in action. And empathy is another critical attribute of founders.

Empathy: A Founder's Superpower

Understanding why people act as they do is critical to connecting with and guiding them. As your children get older, they'll think about what sports they want to play, what instruments they want to learn, what subjects they want to pursue in college—and whether they want to go to college at all. A reliable method for identifying their goals will help your children gain clarity, and it will provide a framework for how you can help them think through those questions. That framework is built over years filled with engagement, questions and answers, dialogue, and learning together. If you provide those from a young age, you'll set your kids up for success no matter what path they choose in life.

And people notice when empathy is missing. Recall that at my company Livescribe, we laid off a third of our employees due to the recession. This is something no good founder ever wants to do, but our hands were tied to assure survival in a financial blizzard. Worse yet, we had limited time to act, which caused me to box up my feelings and rapidly work through these cutbacks (rather than give everyone the attention they needed individually). I lost my personal connection with some of our key people and made some glaring mistakes, missing crucial communication. My assistant, for instance, was on vacation when this all happened, and I neglected calling her to let her know about the layoffs before her return—which painfully included her.

Many employees began to feel disillusioned about our behavior and our company culture. And to be fair, I don't blame them. Our situation was dire with our investors and capital markets, but that didn't mean we shouldn't still do our absolute best by our people. To this day, I regret not doing a better job of acting with more empathy toward my team.

So let me reiterate: People notice when empathy is missing.

Great leaders are able to read people's desires, even those desires that may not be apparent to the person feeling them. Understanding what people want and need is the first step toward creating products that improve your customers' lives—or, in a more general sense, coming up with solutions that people gravitate toward.

You might remember that the idea for an interactive globe arose after I learned that most adults in the United States struggle to identify other countries and even other states. No one likes to feel ignorant, and pride can stop us from admitting what we don't know, so I became committed to launching a product that would help people learn in fun and accessible ways.

I worked with my college roommate from MIT, Mark Flowers, and his colleague, Dave Conroy, to build the Atlasphere globe using touch-sensing technology, radio frequencies, multimodal interaction, and an understanding of human nature. When someone touched the stylus to a country, the globe would respond with music and fascinating facts about that particular place. The core technology powering the globe was groundbreaking. But we realized early on that people weren't going to buy the Atlasphere because of its cool sensing abilities. They needed to respond emotionally when using it.

One evening, Mark, Dave, and I introduced an early prototype to Mark's dad, Bob. Mark and Dave explained their different approaches to building the underlying technology, and Mark's dad acknowledged that the concept was interesting. But he wasn't exactly itching to use it.

Then he spotted a cardboard globe I had cobbled together and "wired" by connecting a few simple switches to a Mac desktop. I spaced the switches around the globe and marked them with red dots to indicate clickable locations. "What's this?" Mark's father asked, his curiosity finally piqued.

"Would you like to try it?" I asked enthusiastically. "Just find as many countries as possible as fast as you can." I clicked "start" on the Mac, and the computer rattled off a list of countries for Bob to find. The music accompanying the game gained tempo as time went on, prompting Bob to respond faster and faster. He did well, up until the Mac asked him to rapidly identify several African countries, and he lost on Burkina Faso.

"I know where Burkina Faso is!" he said. "There must have been something on my glasses…" He rubbed at his frames, ensuring that they wouldn't thwart him on his second round. "Can I try again?" Mark's father felt a small bruise to his ego when he missed Burkina Faso—contrasted with the pride he felt while correctly selecting the other countries the globe prompted him to identify.

That's the night Explore Technologies won over its first investor. It's also when I learned an important lesson about inspiring people to follow you into the abyss of entrepreneurship. Founders might have the most cutting-edge technology and the most foolproof go-to-market strategy—but neither of those matter if they cannot connect with people emotionally. Before founders can ask people to risk their time, income, and ego on their idea, they need to give people a reason to believe in it and establish some form of emotional connection to the business's outcome.

Once founders earn that buy-in, they must sustain it through fair and transparent policies and ongoing attention to the needs of their many stakeholders. Keeping that many people satisfied requires a high level of emotional intelligence that is rooted in skills developed in childhood.

How to Raise Empathetic Kids

Cultivating empathy is a lifelong endeavor rooted, fortunately, in evolutionary brain development; we feel more deeply for others the more we learn about the world. But you'd be surprised at how astute and outwardly minded your kids will be, even at a young age, if you consistently guide them toward empathetic behavior and awareness. Kids who empathize with others tend to be better-adjusted socially than their more aloof or self-interested peers. They're also more likely to stand up for what they believe in and to rally their friends and classmates around important issues.

Put simply, empathy is defined as "the action of understanding, being aware of, being sensitive to, and vicariously experiencing the feelings, thoughts, and experience of another" (according to Merriam-Webster).

While it's true that anyone (with neurotypical brain development) can learn to be empathetic, children are naturally attuned to the world around them. Newborn babies respond instinctively to facial expressions, and research shows that we all display universal cues to indicate emotions, such as happiness, sorrow, disgust, and anger. (See Paul Ekman's Facial Action Coding System.)[1] As we grow older, we sometimes become so absorbed in our own concerns that we lose touch with the feelings of people around us. But children are more attentive to their environments. What better time than to harness their innate empathy than when they are at their most eager and impressionable?

When Blake was 11, one of the other boys in his class was frequently bullied. As is often the case, much of the harassment took place in the locker room, out of sight of any teachers. The chief bully and his hangers-on would tease this boy, who was shy and a little overweight, threatening to pull his pants down in front of his classmates. Now, Blake wasn't exactly a heavyweight. One threatening move from these bullies, and he would have been in trouble. But as he watched his classmate shrink from the daily torment, he felt he couldn't stay silent.

"When you're not popular, people don't want to be associated with you. It's almost an element of toxicity," Blake noted when we reflected on this. Given the social cost, he knew that no one else would speak up for this boy. But Blake empathized with the emotional pain his classmate must have felt suffering this daily harassment, and he decided to speak up.

"Hey, leave him alone!" he finally said to the bully. "Why are you doing this to him? Just back off." Blake recalled that the bully seemed stunned that someone had dared question him, but he did stop teasing the unpopular child. It was a deft approach, because not only did Blake call attention to the bullied boy's suffering, but he also challenged the bully's need to hurt people in the first place.

Blake's willingness to speak up meant a lot to the other boy, whose mom was in tears when she told MJ the story after the fact. But it was a significant moment for Blake, too, because it's when he learned that having empathy means taking action. It's not enough to learn what other people feel. You also have to do something with that information.

Balancing Thinking With Feeling

You've likely heard of the left-brain, right-brain dichotomy, a theory that became popular for explaining why some people gravitate toward creative pursuits while others seem to operate on logic alone. In recent years, we've learned that the relationship between these instincts is much more complex than this theory suggests—Psychology Today has called it "the poster child for pseudoscience."[2] But it remains a handy metaphor, especially for thinking about founders.

It's sometimes assumed that leaders are mostly analytical, or left-brained. They like to dissect problems by studying the facts and making logic-based arguments. However, people aren't inherently inspired by facts and numbers. We're moved by stories, compelling narratives about bettering lives, overcoming adversity, and changing the world. That's where the right brain comes in.

Brain researcher Jill Bolte Taylor describes the right brain as the in-the-moment side of our minds in a completely captivating, highly emotional TED Talk called "My Stroke of Insight."[3] It's what captures the emotional experience of being alive, and it sparks the feeling that we're intimately connected with every other being on the planet. That sensation is exhilarating and deep, and it motivates some of our most profound creativity. Taylor characterizes our left brain, on the other hand, as thinking linearly and methodically. As our right brain is stimulated with the emotional power of existence, the left is unpacking that experience and categorizing it into neat details. The left brain analyzes and predicts based on the sensory input of its right-side counterpart.

The combination of the two halves of our brain is what makes us such cognitively fascinating creatures, and it's what drives our decisions. Common knowledge once told us that people were either emotional and impulsive *or* strictly calculating.[4] But modern science has proven otherwise. Just because an ad or event stirs nostalgia or joy or envy doesn't mean we're going to act on those feelings. Nor does a rational argument necessarily mean we're going to make the best on-paper choices. We draw on both faculties to make decisions, and the better we understand both sides of our brains, the better we are at managing ourselves and connecting with others. For further reading, Daniel Kahneman, the Nobel Prize-winning behavioral economist presents a wonderful model along these lines for thinking, biases, and understanding in his book, *Thinking, Fast and Slow*.[5]

The question is, how do you teach your children to maximize the full power of their intellect and creativity? Like most important lessons, the learning begins with you. Although children are naturally empathetic, they hone that instinct by observing how you behave. By modeling empathy and thoughtfulness and discussing your actions with your children, they'll learn to apply both reason and emotion to all aspects of their lives.

Here are a few ways to practice this:

1. Discuss your feelings openly.

Our society has become increasingly appreciative of emotional intelligence. Self-awareness and empathy are highly valued traits, particularly among successful companies and organizations. Take advantage of this trend by sharing your feelings candidly with your children and inviting them to express their emotions with you as well.

Like many families, you might use dinnertime as an opportunity for everyone to recap the highlights of their day. Go a step further by incorporating your emotional experiences as well. If your child performed well on a test, ask her how that made her feel and why she had that reaction. Perhaps she had an argument with a friend and is feeling sad because the conflict remains unresolved. Explore that experience, too. Why does she feel sad? What instigated the fight, and what were the underlying causes? (In other words, what's the ostensible problem, and what's the PTS?) How does she think her friend feels right now? Such conversations help your children think through conflicts, de-escalating their emotions so they can understand the other person's experience and reason out a potential resolution.

Don't be shy about sharing your emotions, too. If you're feeling frustrated about a situation at work, tell your kids about it. Remember, they want to hear about your life outside the home, so let them know what's going on. Explain why you're aggravated, but be sure to acknowledge the other person's side as well. This reinforces the importance of practicing empathy, even when the stakes feel high. You're really teaching your kids to understand *why* people behave in certain ways, which will make them more adept at finding real, meaningful solutions to problems.

2. Educate your kids about body language.

We give physical clues as to what we're feeling every second of the day. Eye contact, posture, fidgeting, how we angle our bodies— all of these are subtle (and sometimes not so subtle) signs of what's going on in our internal worlds. Teaching your kids to pick up on these cues not only makes them more empathetic, but it can also help them diffuse tense and even dangerous situations.

Imagine that your daughter is in class and a couple of kids next to her break into an argument. She notices that one of them has a red face, is breathing heavily, and his hands are balled into fists beneath his desk. Sensing a potential physical confrontation, she might de-escalate the situation by intervening and asking him about a topic she knows interests him or suggesting that he take a walk to the water fountain. A simple, quiet intervention of this kind could prevent both students from coming to blows or suffering emotional embarrassment.

In a professional setting, you need to assess people quickly. The strength of someone's handshake or whether they stifle a yawn during a meeting serve as important signals when you're trying to close a deal or land a new job. You want to be able to read people quickly, picking up on even the smallest details so you can tailor the tone of your conversation to keep them engaged. People drop hints about what they're feeling or what motivates them all of the time; you just have to know what to watch or listen for.

We'll talk about strategies for teaching body language in the next section. But before we move on, it's worth noting that you can help your kids become aware of the physical messages they send, too. If they're in the habit of crossing their arms and hunching their shoulders, they might come off as insecure or standoffish. A tendency to slouch or walk with their heads down might belie the vibrant personality you know and love. Teaching your kids to use what researcher Amy Cuddy calls "power posing"—using posture to demonstrate confidence and authority—will help them communicate that they have ideas and value to share and that they're eager to participate in what's going on around them without even saying a word.[6] More importantly, power posing will affirm those messages in their own minds. As Cuddy shared in her 2012 TED Talk, how we conduct ourselves physically informs the type of people we become.

MJ and I taught our kids to always look people in the eye and offer them a firm handshake. We observed their physical behaviors when interacting with people, and if we noticed that they crossed their arms, slouched, or put an unusual amount of distance between themselves and someone else, we'd ask them about it later—not to judge or criticize, but to understand and help them become aware of their own instincts. Oftentimes, Blake and Annie didn't even realize they were doing these things until we pointed them out. Then we'd have interesting discussions about the messages they were conveying through that language.

Pay attention to your own mannerisms in the next days and weeks. How often do you cross your arms or shift your weight or look away during a conversation? See whether you can map these behaviors to your feelings. Are you bored? Annoyed? Anxious to move on to your next task? Adjusting your habits to better reflect your feelings will help you teach your children to do the same.

3. Help your kids work through the darker side of human nature.

As an adult, you know not everyone is going to be nice. But when kids are taught to always act kindly and to think of others, it's jarring when they see someone act in a way that's mean or thoughtless; to kids, it can seem unbelievable.

For example, when Blake was 5 years old, we were at a hotel pool when a boy we didn't know asked to play with Blake's favorite toy, a cute dolphin squirt gun. Blake was a sharer and naturally said yes. But when, some time later, we realized both the boy and the dolphin were nowhere to be found, Blake was heartbroken—and to be honest, I was, too. It's a situation nearly every child will face at some point: "I know not to do this, so why would someone else do it to me?" And it's exactly this type of situation that has the potential to bruise kids' trust in others.

There were multiple avenues we could have taken—we could have angrily sought out the family or made Blake out to be a victim in the situation (and as a parent, it's a painful situation, one that tempts us to lash out in defense of our children). But we know that incidents like this are a reality, and we have the responsibility to impart that knowledge to our children.

Have conversations about honesty, intentions versus outcome, and the simple fact that different people behave differently. In our case, we had numerous discussions over these topics; we didn't want Blake to think we were making light of his situation, and we also didn't want this to affect him more than it needed to. Painful as these experiences may be for children, they're going to happen—adult or child, founder or otherwise.

Bottom line: Kids are going to get their feelings hurt and their toes stepped on (especially if they're going out on a limb to found something new). But should they put their guard up to the world simply because not everyone has the right intentions? Absolutely not.

4. Seek opportunities to put empathy into practice.

Empathy should be an ongoing conversation, but it's always best to put what you teach into action. Class presentations are a great opportunity for this. Today, Blake is an extremely animated CEO. When he talks about the work his company is doing, you can't help but get caught up in the excitement and passion that emanate from his every word. But this wasn't always the case.

As a student, Blake was highly logical, and he built class presentations around the facts. His approach was analytical and direct, and while his clarity was impressive in a child, it wasn't exactly engaging at times. Unfortunately, you see this disconnect in many founders, too. They believe that if they present the logical case for why their products are worth buying or investing in, people will be persuaded by reason alone. But as we learned earlier, we're driven by a combination of logic and emotion. A presentation that lacks emotion and narrative is a snooze-fest whether you're in the boardroom or the classroom.

Knowing this, I encouraged Blake to empathize with his classmates whenever he had to create a presentation. Why should they care about the topic he was speaking about? How did these facts connect to their lives? What story could he tell to draw them into the subject? Facts should always provide the foundation, but you need an emotional hook to grab people's attention. As both he and Annie went through school, we really worked with them to hone this skill. When either of them gives a presentation today, their genuine passion lights up the room, and it's because they care about the material and know what matters to their audiences.

5. Discuss guilt management.

There's a fine line between empathy and guilt. Empathy requires that you put yourself in another person's shoes and get inside their mind to understand what they're thinking and feeling and why. But doing so sometimes inspires guilt. If you're in an argument with a friend, you might feel that you've wronged him or that you need to take responsibility for his feelings. When empathizing with customers or clients, you may go overboard trying to solve the world's problems instead of creating something that will have impact for them right now.

When guilt goes unchecked, it can debilitate kids (and founders) due to misplaced doubt, anxious energy, and internal conflict. But when managed properly, guilt can serve as a catalyst for action. Discuss guilt through the lens of your family's religious traditions or the philosophical ideas that underpin your life. Make sure your children see guilt as an instructive emotion for recognizing when they've erred and how they can learn from those mistakes, without allowing it to overwhelm them and make them fearful of taking action in the future.

It's important that children understand how to recognize and respond to self-imposed guilt or the potential use of guilt by someone else. There may be times when a sibling, friend, or colleague wrongs them, and that person may express guilt and a desire to "make it up to them." Explain to your kids that it's fine to accept someone's effort to repair the relationship, but only up to a point. When people hurt us, we're sometimes tempted to hold their past misdeeds over their heads as insurance that they won't do it again. This never works, and the relationship ultimately suffers for it. Teaching your kids to speak openly about their feelings, especially when they're hurt, will help them feel validated without needing to parcel out justice via guilt-inducing reminders about how someone has wronged them in the past.

The ability to acknowledge mistakes and move on will serve your children well as leaders. Founders who apply guilt as a control mechanism over their employees quickly drive away their hardest-working team members because no one wants to be reminded of their past flaws or feel manipulated. Conversely, founders will, at some point, need to fire employees who aren't meeting expectations—even if they like the employee. Those who can help others learn from their mistakes and energize them to do better in the future, however, forge stronger bonds and inspire better outputs than their guilt-minded counterparts.

Tools, Fun, & Magic Moments

Opportunities abound for helping your children connect with others. But MJ and I have found the following circumstances particularly advantageous for imparting lessons about empathy:

1. When you're expecting company:

Having guests over is a great way for kids to learn body language and social cues. Before a colleague or friend arrives for dinner, tell your kids who the person is and what his or her relationship is to you. Share the person's hobbies and career highlights so your kids have something to draw on for sparking a conversation. You're teaching them to be sensitive, respectful, and engaging toward visitors, rather than offering a quick greeting and ignoring them for the rest of the night.

Review proper handshake technique as well. Research shows that a strong handshake indicates confidence. A palm down shake signals dominance, palm up hints at submissiveness, and a weak shake points to uncertainty and insecurity. (Note that these signals depend on cultural context, and I'm speaking from the Western viewpoint). I taught Annie and Blake the shake-and-gaze technique, which is a strong handshake combined with sustained eye contact. Holding another person's gaze for a few seconds creates a sense of familiarity that fosters comfort and trust. After our guests left our house, I liked to ask my kids about their experiences. How did they feel after meeting these new people? Did their actions inspire warmth and friendliness? Or did the other person seem uncomfortable or disinterested? These conversations taught them to reflect on how simple greetings could set the tone for an entire evening.

Once we had done our new-guest postmortems, we would ask Annie and Blake what they learned about our guests. Did they make an effort to get to know our visitors? What had they done to make them feel welcome in our home? The goal was to get our kids paying attention to other people's needs. Perhaps they offered to refill a guest's iced tea if it was running low, or they offered to bring a sweater if the person commented that it was chilly. These seemingly small gestures make a big impression, and the habit of anticipating people's needs is a valuable one for future founders to cultivate.

2. When you're watching movies and TV shows:

Earlier, I shared Annie's reflection that the movie reviews we did after watching films helped her write book reports in middle school. But movies and TV programs offer powerful platforms for cultivating empathy as well. Disney and Pixar, in particular, create movies that are rich in character development and emotion. There's no end to the interesting conversations you can have with your kids about why Woody was so determined to make it home to Andy in *Toy Story* or what was so moving about Carl's and Russell's bond in *Up*. *WALL-E* is really fun for dissecting body language and nonverbal cues, as the main robots don't really talk. *James and the Giant Peach* is a classic film about confronting your fears. You'll be amazed at the evolution of your kids' insights as they mature and at how differently they interpret characters' feelings after watching the same movies over and over again.

You can practice the same habits with TV shows, whether fictional sitcoms or nightly news specials. Most kids tune out when they see a "boring" politician on TV. But you can keep them interested by asking what they perceive those people to be feeling or to imagine what it's like to have so many reporters asking questions at the same time. Querying your children on the body language of politicians or news anchors also invokes powerful discussion. There are countless ways to start conversations with your kids when you're bonding over media and entertainment. It's easy to dismiss movies and TV as just that—entertainment. But the stories your kids watch can profoundly impact their perspectives.

3. When you're in the mood to be silly:

Speaking of narratives, try creating some as a family. The storytelling game mentioned in the previous chapter encourages kids to be playful and share their creativity while also becoming more comfortable with public speaking. As they see how your family members respond to their contributions, whether that's with a giggle or a loving groan, they'll learn what makes a good story and what causes people to tune out.

The Llama Game is another favorite storytelling pastime in our family. As with the storytelling game, every person gets to add a sentence or a word to the story. But in this case, you replace every word with the single word, "llama." So if your sentence is, "One night, in a dark, scary forest, a night owl screamed, 'Hoot,'" you'd repeat "llama" 12 times in lieu of those words—only the inflections and cadence of your voice will give away the tone of the story, and the next person follows suit. It's very silly and a lot of fun, and it's an effective method for teaching your kids to pay attention not just to *what* people say, but *how* they say it.

4. When you're reading together:

Continuing the story theme, there's no better way to inspire confidence in your kids than having them read out loud. When they're too young to read on their own, you can read for them, acting out all of the different characters' personalities. Once they're able to chime in, encourage your children to put their own spin on the many voices in their favorite stories. Doing so will help them become confident in their reading and speaking skills, and it will develop their empathetic tendencies as they imagine how each character might think and feel.

Books' content helps exercise empathy, too. The psychologists Emanuele Castano and David Comer Kidd have discovered that reading literary fiction correlates to increased empathy.[7] Ever since Blake and Annie were young, MJ made frequent trips with them to the library to check out classic children's books, such as *Robinson Crusoe*. She liked that these stories both entertained and enriched the kids' minds. Sure, they all enjoyed the act of reading out loud together. But the events of the books raised questions about right and wrong and how to treat other people.

5. When you're having family game nights:

Family game nights are a fun—and surprising—exercise in empathy. Our kids liked to bend the rules however they could, especially when playing games like Scrabble. They'd insist that they could play Latin words or throw in other twists to try to gain an advantage. We had some spirited arguments over many a game board, but it was all in good fun. Eventually, we'd agree on a set of rules, not realizing in the moment that we had been listening and catering to one another's feelings while negotiating our own positions—a founder-centric skill if ever there was one.

Texas Hold'em, or any variation of poker, is really fun for teaching your kids to be aware of their emotions and of what others are thinking. Annie used to have a terrible poker face; she'd get her cards and let out a loud, dejected sigh. We taught her that being more conscientious about her reactions would help her in the game, and she quickly became a pro at learning how to discreetly restrain her dismay at a bad hand.

As parents, MJ and I saw our empathy tested on more than a few occasions. MJ will tell you that we're a very competitive family, and not one of us loses easily (even in the interest of our kids' happiness). We didn't want our kids to think games were only worth playing if they could win, so we emphasized the experience over the outcome. But we also wanted to bolster their confidence and assure them that they could beat Mom and Dad once in a while. We had to balance our own desire to play all-out with watching our kids' reactions and knowing when to pull back so they could lay claim to the bragging rights from time to time. I remember teaching Annie the simple strategy of Scrabble (to build words around the highest point-making colored squares) and Boggle (to systematically scour the letter cubes looking for shorter, then longer words). She now consistently beats MJ and me at nearly every Jumble game we play. I couldn't be more delighted with this outcome.

6. When you're sharing your favorite books:

Most parents have read a book that's changed their life or at least moved them profoundly. For me, that book is Jim Stovall's *The Ultimate Gift*, a brief but beautiful novel. The premise is that a young man learns that his wealthy uncle, Red, has left him an inheritance, but he can only claim it if he completes a series of 12 tasks during the next year. Each month, Red's lawyer plays a videotape for the nephew instructing him on what to do. The tasks are associated with the important pillars in life, such as family, love, and learning. I strongly recommend sharing it with your children. We read this book aloud to our children, with predictable happy tears streaming down our faces, numerous times. I have also given this book to dozens of my employees in my companies, who have appreciated it for themselves and for their children.

But chances are you have your own life-changing, chill-giving book, too. Make an occasion of sharing that book with your children, whether that means reading it aloud together or passing down a copy for them to read on their own. Ask how they're liking it—what characters stick out to them and why? What events shocked them? How did they feel during (and after) reading it? Remember, works of fiction are good for developing emotional intelligence. But luckily, this "task" is as fun as it is valuable.

Empathy Begins With the Self

I'll end this chapter with a note, and a story, about why empathy for ourselves matters just as much as empathy for other people. You can't really feel for others until you know yourself deeply and understand your own emotions. But more importantly, empathizing with yourself and being able to work through your own feelings is closely tied to the founder's reflective nature. I'll let Annie take it from here:

This past year has been my best year for running competitively, and this past spring, I ran a very competitive 10K (6.2 miles, or 25 laps around the track). For a brief moment, I ranked first in the nation, though I quickly fell further down the list. To qualify for nationals, you have to be in the top 22. Although I was no longer No. 1, I was still placed within the qualifying range.

A couple weeks before the deadline for entering the national race, my team went to one of the last-chance meets. My coach decided that I was likely safe and decided not to have me race the 10K that night. I ran a 5K, which was a much shorter distance, and I ran a great time. Then I came out to watch the 10K, and five girls qualified, putting me in 23rd. I was one spot away from going to nationals.

I was happy for my teammates, but it was very challenging to maintain a positive attitude knowing that I had been so close to being able to race.

The following week, there was a last-last-chance race in Chicago. Running a 5K the week before a 10K is usually inadvisable, but I knew this was my very last possible shot. After talking with Mom, I realized I would regret not taking the opportunity to run this race.

I drove up to Chicago from St. Louis and went into the race with a really positive mindset. But the race was horrible. The optimal temperature for running is about 50 degrees; that day, it was 80 degrees in Chicago with 30 mph winds. My pace was slow, and the run was painful. I spent a good five miles running on my own, and I knew halfway through that I wasn't going to qualify. But I finished. I was happy that I completed the race without passing out, and I was proud that I had the grit to run it, even though I knew my chances of qualifying were slim.

Upon reflection, missing the chance to compete at nationals was absolutely disappointing. But I would have regretted not doing everything I could to be there, and I was glad to be there on the sidelines. I was there for the team and for each of my teammates who were running. I cheered with complete enthusiasm and excitement for my teammates who had qualified.

I may be biased (she is my daughter, after all), but I believe Annie's story exemplifies an empathetic character. She knew herself well enough to anticipate feeling disappointed and regretful if she didn't do everything she could to make it to the national race. But when it became clear that her dream was out of reach, she focused on what she had already achieved and supported her teammates without reservation. Children who grow up knowing how to cope with their feelings display an emotional maturity conducive to them becoming—you guessed it—founders.

Chapter 5
How to Lead

You know how founders think and how they feel. Those two concepts combined—plus a few other essential qualities—bring us to leadership. No matter what their end goal may be, all founders are leaders, so knowing how to effectively lead others is necessary to becoming a great founder. There's no reason why adults can't hone their leadership skills, but you'll be giving your children a tremendous gift by imparting these traits early on.

In short, what does leadership look like? I define founding leaders as individuals whose behavior is inclined to risk-taking and who are resilient, confident, forward-thinking, and thoughtful of others. Each of these is essential to developing great leadership. We're going to dive into what makes a leader, more specifically, from having confidence to taking risks to learning how to accept failure. In this chapter, you'll learn easy ways to encourage these traits in your children as they grow.

Leadership Requires the Confidence to Be Independent (Even When It Scares You, Parents)

If you didn't know what you were capable of, what your potential is, would you be confident enough to lead others? Most people—and most kids, especially—aren't. That's why it's so essential for kids to discover how capable they are in their ability to achieve what they set their mind to. And that's another reason to teach kids to be accountable for their failures: It strengthens their overall independence and builds confidence in the face of the unknown. Children who repeatedly expose themselves to new experiences and failure are secure in their abilities. They're less fearful because they've been in tough situations and made it through, and they know they can rely on themselves even when they're frightened or frustrated. I like to call this "stacking successes"—creating a cushion of achievements to bolster confidence in taking on the next risk with aplomb, humility, and passion.

Independence and confidence aren't only born of hardship, however. Simply being in unfamiliar or uncomfortable situations can help cultivate children's problem-solving abilities—and more importantly, their confidence in those abilities. This can happen in large and small ways. For instance, parents are sometimes fearful of letting their kids go on long, unsupervised bike rides with their friends. Parents worry that their kids will get lost or hurt, so they attempt to keep them close to home. But again, this well-intentioned boundary hinders kids' growth. Instead of trying to keep them in your sight at all times, start riding bikes with them at a young age. Emphasize the importance of wearing a helmet (and practice what you preach). Ask your kids to review safety measures, such as looking both ways and keeping to bike paths and lanes, while you're out riding together. And if necessary, equip them with a phone for tracking, if you feel so inclined.

Then, once they're old enough, give kids a little more freedom every year. It's tough to let go, but they need to become self-reliant (on *and* off a bike). Being able to explore the neighborhood and beyond with friends is a rite of passage, not to mention a great opportunity for children to stretch their boundaries and see what they're capable of. If they get lost, they'll need to problem-solve on how to get home. If they get a flat tire, they'll have to figure out the best way to cope. These are uncomfortable situations, but if you've guided your children up to that point, they'll be able to draw on that knowledge and find solutions. You'll be amazed at how their confidence and self-esteem will grow as they realize that they can, in fact, take care of themselves and that they're capable of solving problems on the fly.

Resilience-building opportunities crop up more as your kids grow, which is bittersweet. It's thrilling to see your children blossom, but it's also difficult to realize they don't need you as much as they once did. Blake was in middle school the first time he flew on a plane without MJ and me. He had traveled with us in the past, so he was familiar with airplanes, but a cross-country flight without your parents is a big deal to a kid (and to his mom and dad). Blake knew the people meeting him at the airport, and we went over his travel plans and emergency contingencies several times before he boarded. But ultimately, we had to let him walk the bridgeway alone, and he had to summon the courage to do it. Despite the question marks that always arise with air travel—What if the flight is delayed? What if he gets nervous on the plane? What if the airport is difficult to navigate?—Blake walked confidently onto the plane. He knew he could handle the trip, and he did so marvelously. From then on, he walked a little taller, his self-assuredness reinforced by this accomplishment.

We saw Annie's leadership skills emerge with confidence-building challenges as well. In Chapter 2, I shared how Annie and I worked together to find the problem to solve (PTS) when she asked me to help her sell Girl Scout Cookies. But there's another side to that story—as you might imagine, switching up cookie sales wasn't as easy as deciding to do something different and moving right ahead with it. So after Annie decided to sell homemade cookies instead of those offered by the organization, she had to approach her troop leaders to get approval for the idea. Pushing back against the status quo isn't easy even under the friendliest circumstances, but young Annie summoned her courage and made a great pitch to her leaders.

I know it wasn't the most comfortable conversation she ever initiated. However, it was a great learning experience. Annie explained why she didn't want to sell Girl Scout Cookies and outlined her alternate plan. She also assured her troop leaders that her approach didn't require any extra effort on the leaders' part, which is a key persuasion point when lowering the barrier to new ideas. Her troop leaders got on board, and before long, Annie had raised enough money to meet her quota and be eligible for the prizes she desired as part of the cookie campaign. Through finding an alternative to the status quo, presenting her idea, and making a compelling case for it, Annie got her first taste of what it is to be a leader.

By the time she was in high school, Annie's leadership qualities were already on full display. Like Blake, she became head of the award-winning school newspaper and even initiated charitable activities among her friends.

In the summer prior to her junior year, Annie applied to attend the Tony Robbins Global Youth Leadership Summit, a four-day program that provides students ages 14 to 17 with an "environment designed to boost them into leadership roles that will change their lives and communities." To our delight, Annie was accepted! The leadership program evokes the deepest, most profound feelings and desires in people and brings participants face-to-face with themselves in a manner that can propel kids to pursue and achieve their potential. I highly encourage participation in this program for your teenager; the program is open to students around the world and offers scholarships. This was a life-changing event for Annie, as it exposed her to students from around the world who shared their anxieties, hopes, and dreams. After one week, Annie returned with a much deeper understanding of her place in the world, her privileges, and the needs of others at all socio-economic levels.

In college, Annie grew her Bear Cubs organization and led several other campus groups. Exposing her to early opportunities to pursue and defend her ideas created resilience and confidence to lead in a variety of capacities.

A Note on Popularity

You don't need me to tell you that popularity is not equivalent to leadership—but when you're in school, it's easy to feel like the popular kids are the ones with all the influence. And when kids believe social clout lies in the hands of the few, it's easy to want to take a back seat. We see this as early as middle school, when kids (girls in particular) stop raising their hands during class or stop sharing their ideas because they're afraid of social ostracism. Boys suffer in this way as well, but the problem is especially rampant among girls.

Rosalind Wiseman's book *Queen Bees and Wannabes* focuses on this exact topic, unveiling the labyrinthine politics that seem to crop up among girls starting in middle school.[1] If a young girl is going to risk the approval of the popular kids by pursuing an idea she's passionate about, she needs to feel supported in some corner of her life.

Both parents and children tend to mistake popularity for leadership, but the two are not one and the same. In fact, leadership often requires a willingness to take a stand for unpopular people or ideas. However, it's often the popular kids who get voted into student government roles or other presumed leadership positions. If your child isn't one of the popular students, she may discount herself as a leader. But there are many ways to lead, including in our everyday behaviors. She can start new clubs, introduce interesting ideas to her friends, and band together with other kids to stand up to a schoolyard bully. Kids who take initiative regardless of whether they have an "official" title are the ones who grow up to lead.

Becoming Best Friends With Risk

Leaders are risk-takers, whether the risk is large or small; simply getting the courage to rally others around a common goal can feel risky. In order for kids to become strong leaders, they need to get comfortable with risk—and parents need to let them.

We've discussed it before, but it's worth reiterating: When parents give children a simple "no" with little to no reasoning following it—even for their own good—they limit the feelings of growth and confidence that accompany the risk of new experiences. You may have good reasons for not wanting your children to ride their bikes at night or to warn them about experimenting with their chemistry sets. But the lack of exposure to these experiences and your perceived lack of confidence in them will make kids fearful of new opportunities. It will also make them second-guess their abilities because they never had a chance to hone them.

Blake always had a penchant for chemistry, even at 8 years old. An exceptional teacher, Judy Pentopolous, inspired in him a lifelong love of the field, and while other kids were watching cartoons, Blake was off memorizing the periodic table. It wasn't long before he wanted to conduct experiments at home.

I happily supported his chemistry hobby, even allowing him to create gunpowder and hydrogen in our garage, the latter of which caused palpable shock waves when ignited within a balloon. When one of Blake's experiments caught fire in a neighboring field, however, MJ put her foot down. "That's it," she said. "No more chemical experiments. I want these chemicals gone!"

Now, I knew I didn't want to deprive Blake from continuing his experiments. For all the reasons just mentioned, I insisted that we find a workable solution. So MJ, Blake, and I discussed the PTS. The ostensible problem was that MJ was worried about Blake's (and the rest of the family's) safety as long as we were bringing potentially dangerous chemicals into the house. But the chemicals weren't the problem. I posited that the PTS was how we were managing Blake's experiments. Surely there was a way we could encourage him without compromising anyone's well-being.

MJ and I agreed that Blake would keep a logbook and document his experiments with the scientific method. Before starting an experiment, we asked that he define the project, write his hypothesis, list the materials he needed, and demonstrate his expected outcomes, creating a protocol to follow before we gave his experiments the green light.

Then in seventh grade, Blake had developed a fascination with sodium, a silver metal that self-combusts and explodes when exposed to moisture or air! He had spent weeks watching videos of sodium experiments, getting increasingly excited as he watched 30-foot repeated explosions caused by dropping a fist-sized lump of sodium into a lake. Blake's enthusiasm was infectious, and I allowed him to use my credit card to purchase sodium online. I figured it was money well spent if it furthered his chemistry education. (If we're being honest, I had watched the videos myself and was becoming a little curious, too....)

As it would turn out, Blake wasn't the only one who learned from the great sodium experiment. A few days after he placed the order, I found Blake waiting at the door for me when I arrived home from work. He was smiling, but I could tell something was wrong (via that parental sixth sense we all know too well). "Hi, Dad," he grinned with reserve. "The sodium arrived!" He led me to our kitchen table, on which sat a cardboard box about eight inches wide, six inches high, and six inches deep, printed with the warning "DO NOT GET WET. THIS SIDE UP." Blake reopened the box and withdrew two silvery three-inch diameter, eight-inch long solid tubes of grayish, shiny metal sealed in thick plastic bags, containing some type of clear, oily liquid. Together the tubes weighed 5 pounds. We had *5 pounds* of sodium in our kitchen.

"Don't worry, Dad. I've got it figured out," Blake offered, gauging my stunned, speechless response. "We'll go to the hardware store, buy some coolers, and fill them with kerosene. We'll immerse the sodium in kerosene and leave the coolers in the garage. It'll be safe."

For all of his experience with chemical reactions, Blake was unfamiliar with kerosene. But I grew up around the stuff and knew it was highly flammable. I told him that submerging the sodium in kerosene in our garage was not an option, but there wasn't much we could do at the moment. We had to leave for his Scouts meeting, and I didn't want MJ to know about the situation just yet. I hadn't told her about the sodium purchase to begin with, and it hardly seemed fair to tell her as we were running out the door.

While at the Scouts meeting, I saw my friend Richard, a chemist. "We've got some new chemicals," I told him. Richard was always interested in Blake's experiments.

"Oh yeah? What did you get?" he asked.

"Well..." I was a little embarrassed to admit our predicament. "We got some sodium."

Richard raised his eyebrows as his eyes popped open. "*Sodium?*" he said as impressed as he was startled. "How much?!"

"Five pounds," I said flatly.

Richard's jaw dropped. He froze. He stared at me as though I had gone mad. "Five pounds?!" he paused. Then again, "Five pounds?! You can't keep that in your house! If there's an earthquake and the fire department comes and sprays your house, you'll blow up your neighborhood!"

Needless to say, the ride home with Blake was one of the more tense moments that's ever occurred between us. Sternness, judgement, and practicality converged in our discussion. We mulled options. Bury it in the backyard? Can't do that. If an animal got to it and scratched the package open—it might catch fire. Throw it in the garbage? Out of the question. Keep it? Blake's momentary appeal motivated another round of stern discussion. When we got to our house, I moved the sodium to a wooden closet in our garage, just beneath our bedroom.

That night, I lay awake, tossing and turning, with the silvery, caustic bomb six feet beneath my head, much to MJ's wonderment. Again, it didn't seem a prudent time to tell her there was a potential bomb in our house.

The next morning, Blake and I made some decisions. We kept a small amount of sodium for Blake's experiments and gave some to his science teacher, who was ecstatic with this gift. Apparently Blake had stumbled onto a remarkably good deal, acquiring thousands of dollars of sodium for $100. Then we called a local hazmat facility to dispose of the rest. The specialist who answered the phone responded similarly to Richard.

When we arrived at the facility, they instructed us to stay in the car. The officials who approached the car were wearing full gas-mask protected yellow rubber bodysuits with sealed gloves; "Stay in the car," they said through their masks with their rubber hands raised. They removed the sodium, which was sealed in Tupperware containers filled with vegetable oil, from the trunk, treating it as gingerly as dynamite, while everyone not involved in the extraction backed far away.

Though this was a harrowing experience, I never condemned Blake for creating the danger or forced him to stop experimenting, even if his actions kept me up all night. We talked about how to proceed with greater caution in the future, and the experience stayed with both of us. If I had simply shut down Blake's experiments—and there were moments I was tempted to do so— he might have lost confidence, lost interest, been resentful, and certainly would have missed future learning experiences. He likely would have beaten himself up for ordering so much sodium, and he'd feel less competent when in the lab at school. Worst of all, he would have taken my reaction as evidence that I didn't trust or believe in him. Mistakes happen in real life, and I wanted Blake to understand how to learn from them, not fear them.

Plain and Simple: Leaders Fail

Of course, your kids won't always succeed. Their ideas will be rejected, the events they plan will flop, and the clubs they start may attract only a handful of members. Those moments will be emotionally challenging, but they're also prime teaching opportunities. Instead of letting your children wallow in their perceived failures, ask them to list their successes. What worked? What could they have done better? How will they incorporate those lessons next time? Founders and leaders will fail many, many times. It's the forward-thinking mindset that sets them apart. Rather than moping about failures, founders move on to the next endeavor. Oftentimes, they plan to fail bigger the next time around—and still bigger on the next round. It's not so much that they're seeking failure; they're simply acting without the fear of failure.

When your kids do fail, assess setbacks with them, and then help them identify the path forward. In the entrepreneurial world, we do this all the time (at least, we should)—it's called a postmortem (which, in Latin, literally means "after death"). After a project ends—and especially when it ends poorly—teams sit down to evaluate both the project's strengths and its weaknesses, then identify what changes they have in mind for next time. At my companies, we've never failed without knowing why and without understanding what we can improve upon, and that's a practice too good to limit to the world of business.

Of course, watching your kids fail isn't easy (remember how hard it was for me to watch Blake struggle on that hike?). Few things are more heartbreaking than seeing your son's face crumple in tears when he loses a competition or seeing your daughter be passed over for the school play after she spent weeks preparing for auditions. Yet, just like when your child faces teacher problems, you must resist the urge to intervene. This includes everyday instances like homework struggles as well. When you agree to finish your child's algebra problems "just this once," you're really telling her it's not important for her to learn the concepts herself. You must let your kids struggle, no matter how much it pains you. They need to learn how to cope with tough assignments and setbacks; you can't do it for them.

What you *can* do is create a supportive safety net. When your kids fail—and they will, no matter how bright or talented they are—you can meet them with empathy and understanding, as well as help them learn how to treat themselves with their own inner voice of empathy and understanding. You can teach them how to conduct their own postmortems, talking them through what happened, helping them find the lessons in the sadness, and most importantly, helping them see the bright side. Positivity is one of the most valued attributes of effective leaders, so you're doing your kids a great service when you don't let them dwell on the negative. Make it a point to end conversations about failures on a high note. You might apply this to disagreements or discussions of personal problems as well. What's the upshot? If kids frame even disappointments and arguments in a positive light, they'll feel empowered by their experiences, not beaten down.

To put this another way (and we talked about something similar in Chapter 3), do not allow your children to see themselves as victims. As soon as people become a victim in their own mind, they've given up their autonomy and agency. No matter what the outcome, we must own our fates and circumstances. Sure, bad weather might have created less than ideal conditions for the car wash fundraiser your children organized, or getting a cold might have caused them to underperform at an important game or meet. But there are lessons in every setback and opportunities for accountability in all disappointments. Owning our fates and circumstances is one of the first steps toward becoming a leader.

Encouragement Builds Leaders Up

Few things are more upsetting than hearing parents discourage their children. Oftentimes they're trying to correct dangerous or misguided behavior, but the language that many parents use is extremely negative. Phrases such as "Don't ever do that!" or "What could you possibly have been thinking?!" or "How could you be so stupid?" stick with children when they're said by a parent with fear, frustration, anger, or without reasoning.[2] When parents reprimand in this way, they're creating a little voice inside their children's head that will reverberate each time the child tries something new.

If we're not careful, we discourage our children in subtler ways as well. Even if we don't verbally dismiss children's hobbies or interests, ignoring them when they describe their projects is enough to burst their enthusiasm. As parents, our opinions mean everything to our kids. A lack of encouragement has a damning effect on their confidence and can hinder them from exploring new ideas and activities in the future.

Of course, the road to these kinds of parenting habits is paved with good intentions. Parents want the best for their children, and their harshest criticisms stem from a desire to see them succeed. Parents don't take pleasure in telling their kids "No" or "You can't do that," but part of parenting is making tough calls. However, the way you verbalize your decisions and opinions has a lasting effect on your children's development.

Imagine that your 15-year-old daughter asks for permission to participate in a school-sponsored volunteer trip to an underdeveloped country. You research the area where she would be staying and find out that it's in a region ridden with conflict. Your daughter has never left the country, and you feel she's too young and inexperienced for such a trip at this point in her life. Even after getting in touch with the school staff organizing the trip, you're simply not comfortable with the idea. So you tell your daughter, "No, I don't want you taking the trip. It's too risky."

Ostensibly, she may be angry with you for denying her the opportunity to travel and volunteer with her classmates. But there's a far more insidious consequence at play as well. Now that she has it in her head that such a trip is too risky, she may deny herself future opportunities to serve in this way, putting risk before reward even when she's ready for an experience like that.

A more productive approach would be to explain your logic to her and brainstorm a solution together. You don't want her to go on this trip because you feel she's too young and that she lacks the self-defense skills and knowledge of the world to stay safe in this region. But the conversation doesn't have to end there (notice a theme about continuing conversations and discovering the PTS?). Perhaps you can take a self-defense class or survival course together, or you can take time to learn more about the country in question and its issues, as well as how you can support her from afar. That will give you a chance to bond, and it will help you become more comfortable with a situation like this in the future. Or, if you have the financial means, perhaps you can sign up for a volunteer trip together. Then she can cultivate the experience that will help her the next time a school-sponsored trip opens up, and you'll be able to help her learn what to pay attention to and how to respond to dangerous situations.

By collaborating to find a solution instead of saying "no" outright, you're teaching her to think creatively about solving problems—and as we discussed in earlier chapters, that's a core skill of founders.

Leaders Don't Let 'That's Not Fair' Affect Their Thinking

As an adult, you can decide when you want to view life as not "fair." Founders frequently face situations that aren't "fair," by many standards, from being passed over for funding to key employees leaving. When that does happen, to many, it may seem unfair, but it's just business—and really, it's just life. And founders have the choice to let it set them back or to move on (and I'll let you guess which they normally choose).

You'll see this fact of life confirmed again and again as your kids engage with the world. A biased referee makes a blatantly bad call favoring his kid's soccer team. A teacher plays favorites and excludes would-be eager students from interesting classroom opportunities. Witnessing such instances of unfairness evokes anger in many parents. It's hard as a parent. You want your children to have every opportunity in life, and it hurts that you can't always ensure that they have them. But that's reality. You can't control teachers and coaches and bad refs. However, you can control how you *react* to unfairness, particularly in front of your kids.

Let's assume your son loves performing, but after an audition, he loses out on a choir solo to another student. You may be tempted to tell him that the other student's parent is president of the PTA or that the choir director was just playing politics. "It's not you, it's them," you may be tempted to say. That might even be true. But simply commiserating about how life isn't fair doesn't help your son.

When you tell your kids, "It's not fair—you should have won," you train them to make excuses—much like when you let them deem a task impossible. Every time they're cut from the team or they lose a school election, they'll blame everyone but themselves, limiting their ability to step forward and take action and lessening the chance they'll go out on a limb and try again in the future. And if children think the world is against them, they don't have much incentive to try again next time, do they? Simply put, this mindset hinders leadership.

Sometimes kids truly are caught in circumstances of inequitable practices. Even then, however, it's more constructive to dissect what happened together, not blithely condemn it. If a classmate got away with bad behavior or was given the same grade for lesser work, ask your child about the circumstances surrounding his complaints. Then approach the situation with curiosity. "Let's understand what happened" is much more productive than "That's not fair." Then you can lead into, "What will you do differently next time?" Maybe he'll attend after-school tutoring sessions to make sure he's ready for a big math test, or he'll speak up when he sees a classmate misbehaving. These actions won't guarantee a different result, but it helps your child concentrate on what he can do to reassure himself that he's not powerless, and it shifts the focus to how to improve moving forward—and leaders are always looking at how to improve.

Commitments Matter, No Matter How Small

Imagine a boss who frequently says you'll get a raise next quarter but never follows through, or an organization president who is consistently late to scheduled meetings, or a project lead who seems to change what she's asking of you on a whim. Would you want to follow leaders like that? It's unlikely—we want to trust leaders, and that means the leaders need to take their commitments (both large and small) seriously.

Leaders are people of their words, so establish a zero-tolerance policy on flaking in your household. Remember that you set the example for your kids. If you cancel plans with friends at the last minute simply because you don't feel like showing up, you're telling your kids it's acceptable to disrespect other people's time. Illness and emergencies aside, it's best for your kids to see you following through on the things you said you'd do.

This is especially important when it comes to commitments you've made to your children. They can only hear, "Something came up at work" or "I had an important meeting" so many times before they start to believe that you value other things more than spending time with them or supporting them at important events. Your children may then treat other relationships in their lives cavalierly, making plans and then disregarding their friends' feelings when they don't feel like showing up. When true emergencies do arise (as they will), sit with your children and explain the situation. Make sure they understand that your absence truly was a critical decision that you made with their needs deep in your heart and that canceling your plans does not reflect how much you love them. Explain the actions you're taking to prevent such a situation from happening again, or occurring frequently, so they know that you're taking it seriously.

If you consistently honor your commitments, your kids will learn to honor theirs, too. When they inevitably have to break plans or promises, they'll model your behavior and treat that decision with the gravity it deserves. Leaders must keep to their word if they are to lead effectively, and learning this habit starts with those small efforts at home.

> "If you consistently honor your commitments, your kids will learn to honor theirs, too."

Leaders Know White Lies Are Still Lies

Being a person of your word doesn't just mean following through on promises and commitments; it means being honest, too. When people follow your lead, it means they've placed trust in you—and being dishonest breaks that trust.

Kids, as well-intentioned as they are, lie for many reasons. Sometimes it's to avoid trouble, sometimes for entertainment, and sometimes to see how far they can carry a non-truth before they must come clean. They also learn early on how to frame a situation so they aren't technically lying. For instance, you might notice that there are far fewer cookies in the cookie jar than there were this morning. You ask your child, and she swears that no, she didn't eat them. Strictly speaking, that may be true. But she stood and watched as her friend who was visiting helped herself. When you probe deeper, she admits this. "But I didn't eat them!" she insists. She didn't want to get in trouble, so she lied by omission.

Such untruths may seem less harmful than telling outright falsehoods, but do not indulge this practice. Explain that white lies and lies of omission have the same effect as big lies and that all of them make you trust her less. You don't want your children growing up to engage in deceitful practices in their personal or professional lives.

Of course, children learn these behaviors from their parents. Every time you stretch the truth about why you were late for a family gathering or why you've broken plans with a friend, your kids see this and integrate it into their own habits. If you lie to your friends, why can't they lie to theirs? Practice full honesty in front of and with your kids as much as possible, and discuss your reasons for situations where you may choose to spare people hurt or other reasons you might have for behavior which you feel could misguide your children. For instance, when they ask you to play a game you find boring, don't lie and say you're unwell and then go watch TV. Explain that you don't want to do that particular activity but that you'd love to spend time with them doing something else, or be truthful about needing some time to yourself. Share that you had a long day at work and would like to read a book quietly and unwind, but suggest an activity you can enjoy together after dinner. In fact, demonstrating to your children that it's acceptable to set personal boundaries like that is a healthy example for them to see.

Lying to your children not only teaches them that it's OK to deceive people, but it also causes them to doubt you. They might not call you on it, but your kids will begin to wonder whether you're telling the truth on important questions or whether you're just making excuses so you don't have to spend time with them. You can be honest while still looking out for their feelings. Doing so teaches them how to create and enforce their own boundaries while respecting other people as well.

Leaders Aren't Bosses; They're Team Players

Now imagine if you had a supervisor at work who took all the credit for every project your department completed. Sure, he led the project and ensured deadlines were met, but you and your colleagues worked for weeks—perhaps even months—and it wouldn't feel great to pour all that effort into something if it weren't recognized. These people may be someone's boss, but behavior like this is not an indicator of leadership.

This touches on one of the most important lessons I've learned as an entrepreneur: Very rarely (if ever) can success be attributed to one person.

I've had the good fortune to be recognized for a variety of successes in my career, so I've learned the feelings of exuberance and invincibility that can easily emerge following a big success. But I've also learned to view the adulation that may follow as admiration of the *role* I have played on a *team*, rather than of me personally. This allows me to be thankful for praise while simultaneously recognizing the praise as being toward both the contributions made in my role and, more importantly, toward the team as a *whole*.

MJ and I always encouraged Annie and Blake to be team players, not just in their school activities, but at home as well. We wanted our kids to be reliable, trustworthy people, and we often talked about looking out for one another's needs and offering help when we see an opportunity to lend a hand. Whenever we saw an opportunity for our kids to help out their sibling or parent, we would have conversations centering around what it meant to be a team player.

Team player conversations are great opportunities for helping your kids proactively think about what's going on in other people's lives. I encourage you to foster a team player mentality in your own family as well, emphasizing in every situation how each family member's actions fit into the bigger picture. For example, if your son takes on some of your daughter's chores while she struggles to complete an assignment for school, that might free up more time later on for the whole family to spend playing a game or watching a movie together. There is no greater environment for children to learn what it means to support and be supported by others in their immediate community—their home, school, and activities.

You can extend this to your children's friends and classmates as well. At some point in your children's education, they're going to tell you about a "problem" classmate. This person may or may not be a bully; oftentimes, the child is simply disruptive or is frequently sent to the principal's office. Instead of telling your child to steer clear of this student, explore what might be going on for that person. If possible, get context from the teacher or a class parent who can shed light on the student's home environment. Perhaps his parents are going through a divorce and he's struggling with the adjustment. Maybe he's recently learned that he's adopted and is now confused about his identity. Or maybe his family has fallen on hard times so he's having a difficult time focusing at school. Always ask why, promote empathy, and teach your kids to consider context (while they're at it, they'll be putting to use the skills they've learned from the concepts in Chapters 2, 3, and 4).

Help your children understand rather than judge their classmate's behavior. They may even think of ways to support their fellow student, even if it's just through inviting that child to eat lunch together or playing together during free time. If you set the foundation for this kind of empathy and curiosity when your kids are young, they'll carry those traits with them in high school and college, when it's more difficult for you to get information about their peers. This attunement to what's happening in other people's lives will serve them well in their professional pursuits because they'll know how to connect with disparate audiences.

Children who grow up focused solely on their own needs and experiences may become bullies in adolescence and deeply callous leaders as adults. Research shows that power can warp people's brains until they can't effectively assess risk and struggle to view a situation from another person's perspective.[3] Long-time leaders' ability to mirror other people's experiences weakens, and that trait is essential to practicing empathy—which is necessary to leading others effectively. Too much time spent focusing on themselves and their ambitions can severely impair people's abilities to consider other people's needs and feelings. For instance, many people idolize Steve Jobs despite his own empathic shortcomings. Jobs was brilliant. But the many public stories of his outbursts toward his employees—and the ones I've heard from friends who worked with him—are disconcerting and detract from the portrait of him as a great leader.[4] Brilliance and success are not free passes to disregard other people's feelings, and behaving otherwise hurts your relationships.

By teaching your kids to be team players, you instill the values of great founders. They'll grow up to be in tune with the people around them, making them more intuitive leaders and better people all-around.

Tools, Fun, & Magic Moments

You'll find many, many opportunities for helping your kids hone their leadership skills. Sports and other extracurricular activities, of course, should absolutely be part of their lives because they teach discipline and cooperation; getting involved in organizations such as Scouts or school clubs can give rise to many leadership opportunities as well. After Blake's tough hike with the Scouts, he became newly invigorated about his involvement in the organization. He was selected to attend a leadership class and eventually came back as a staff member, helping to develop a curriculum that was adopted by the adult Scout leaders. That was a huge boost to his confidence, and I saw similar effects when he pursued other goals. In karate, Blake earned his black belt and taught other students. Simply by getting involved and exploring his interests, he naturally evolved into a leader.

But there are ways to weave leadership lessons throughout kids' everyday lives as well, not just in two-hour blocks on a particular day after school. The following practices are some of my family's favorite ways to hone the characteristics we've just discussed while still having fun.

1. Practice trust falls.

Trust and faith are essential to risk-taking, and playtime is a great place for teaching your children about trust. Learning that other people are dependable is a key component of childhood development, and trust falls are a fun way to introduce this concept. Ask your child to stand on a slightly raised surface or on a staircase a few steps above you. Have her turn her back to you and then allow herself to fall into your arms. She may be hesitant at first, because forcing yourself to fall backward is counterintuitive. But once she realizes that you're there to catch her, she'll love playing the game.

As your children become more comfortable with it, you might increase the distance between you and them. This will be a little scary for some at first. But again, once they trust that you will catch them, they'll enjoy it even more, and you'll get a lot of joy out of this simple game. The Boy Scouts play a variation of trust falls called Wind in the Willows. One person stands in the center of a circle and then allows himself to fall in any direction, trusting that his fellow Scouts will catch him.[5] That's an advanced version that you may want to introduce when your kids are a bit older or when they have friends visiting the house.

Annie still recalls playing the trust fall game on our back porch and in the stairs inside our house. She said that being able to look in my eyes and then have me catch her as she fell reinforced the trust between us. She put her confidence in me as her father and as a leader because she believed I would be there for her. That's a very powerful bond to establish between you and your kids.

2. Involve your kids in your work.

I spoke earlier about the importance of talking to your kids about your work. But I also recommend—if you're able—bringing them to work throughout their childhood. Of course, not everyone will be able to do this, but there are still ways to share your work with your children. If you work in food service, for instance, you're likely unable to bring your kids to sit in. But if a partner or friend is able to bring your children up for a meal, that's a great way to involve your kids in what you do. And when your kids are older, you can encourage them to seek an internship or part-time job at your company if possible. You want to avoid nepotism, of course, but if your organization offers an internship or summer work program, suggest that they apply. They'll learn a great deal from seeing you at work, and the experience will foster confidence in themselves as they navigate a professional workplace.

Blake once held an internship at Livescribe, so he got to sit in on our weekly meetings and see how I led our discussions. He also was able to listen in on the office gossip about me when people forgot that my son was in the office and were loose with their comments. That was interesting for both of us, although I asked Blake not to share anything he heard until he completed his internship, and then I used negative comments to simply help me understand myself and others better. Whenever I could, I invited Blake to see different aspects of the business. He once visited QVC with me when I was there for a business meeting, and he joined me with some of my team members to assist us when I spoke at the Aspen Institute. These were incredible learning and bonding experiences, and I encourage you to seek as many opportunities as possible to share your work with your children.

Many parents assume that they can't bring their children to meetings and on business trips, but you'd be surprised at how receptive people are to such requests. Unless the meetings are extremely confidential, I've found most people are happy to accommodate your children, so long as they're old enough to know not to disrupt meetings and discussions. Of course, it's up to you to make the experience interesting. If you relegate them to an empty conference room with nothing to do, they won't gain any value. But if your kids get to sit with you and watch you negotiate or work through problems with colleagues, they'll learn a tremendous amount about how to think and create; they'll also learn about who you are outside of being their parent.

These opportunities don't need to cease when your kids graduate from high school. I've recently had the good fortune to do presentations jointly with both Blake and Annie at professional conferences and entrepreneurship events. We both spoke at the same events and coordinated our notes and the "behavioral change" that we wanted to achieve in our speaking. Initially, both children expressed intimidation because I've been working in the field and speaking so long on technology and innovation, while they're at the beginning of their careers. But it was incredibly rewarding to develop the presentations together and see how our perspectives complemented one another. Blake and Annie discovered that they had much more knowledge and experience to share than they realized, and it was hugely rewarding and fun to collaborate as both family members and professionals.

3. Let your kids speak for themselves while out to eat.

The next time you want to take the family out to dinner, request that your young children order for themselves. Don't worry if they're only 5 or 6 years old; that's the perfect time to initiate the habit. They'll likely be a little intimidated at first, and that's OK. You can practice with them before the server comes over, going through what your children should say. This is a simple way to get them comfortable talking with adults in safe ways and helps them refine their communication skills as they need to present the information in a clear way in order to achieve a desired outcome. Those small building blocks of clear, effective communication prepare your kids for interactions throughout their adulthood.

4. Make your kids your navigators when getting from point A to point B.

Leadership requires confidence, and letting your children take over a task like navigation is one small but effective way to help build that confidence. If your family owns a car, you can have them take over giving directions; if you use public transportation, you can look at the map together, identify where your starting and ending points are, and let your kids determine which route to take and what time a bus or train will arrive. You may not want to do this when you're running late or have a deadline for arriving somewhere. But the next time you have free time and you're on the road, ask your kids to direct you to the store or home. Don't correct them if they tell you to turn down the wrong street or choose a route that sets you back by 20 minutes. Let yourself get lost, and then work together to find your way home.

Although smartphones make it very easy to find your way just about anywhere, knowing how to navigate without technology is an important skill. More importantly, it stretches your kids' brains to recall what they know about directions and orientation. Eventually, they'll gain confidence as they realize they can navigate even in unfamiliar terrain—a metaphorical leadership lesson as much as a practical one.

5. Write contracts to negotiate squabbles.

Occasionally, when Blake and Annie fought (which, like most siblings, varied in frequency across their youth), MJ and I directed them to hash it out together, and we taught them how to write a contract to define their future roles or agreed-upon resolution. This was a simple way for us to reinforce the principle that, when conflicts arise, we must find a solution and—just as importantly—we absolutely must honor the solution we've come to.

At times, we would sit down together and outline, in writing, the essentials: what the behavior was, why it was upsetting the other sibling, what the "terms" were (the solution), and what the consequences were if those terms were broken. Blake and Annie often asked MJ and me to police the contracts and enforce the agreed-upon consequences if one of them violated the terms. But they had to identify the PTS, and they had to decide on the terms with each other. Having that written document also came in handy when we encouraged them to follow through on their promises; if a certain behavior reappeared only days later, we could all refer back to the contract to understand both what we said we would (or wouldn't) do and *why* we agreed on those terms.

You can take this beyond sibling fights, too, of course. If a child is having a behavior problem with you, your partner, other family members, or family friends, apply the same principles.

MJ and I chose to do this because we knew that simply telling our kids to stop fighting or admonishing one for antagonizing the other was ineffective. How many times have you repeated the phrases "Don't tease your sister" or "Stop annoying your brother," only to have your words fall on deaf ears? Outlining something specific—and something you as a family can refer back to—can help.

No matter who the conflict lies between, hammering your kids with threats and pleas often doesn't work, especially not in the long run. But giving them the tools to work out their problems among themselves teaches children important life skills and keeps the responsibility with them.

Chapter 6
How to Found

Now is when it all comes together. You know the bedrock principles that go into the founder's mindset. You know how founders think, how founders feel, and how founders lead. The natural next step is learning that last step that truly cements a person as a founder—how to turn an idea into a reality, or how to found.

During the past decade, our culture has come to associate the word "founder" with Silicon Valley startups. There are a lot of founders in the Bay Area, but I believe that's too narrow an interpretation of the word. Founders can be anywhere, especially among kids. Children are natural founders. The inclination to set up a lemonade stand, go house to house offering to pet sit or mow lawns, post flyers offering babysitting services, or even start a new club at school are all examples of founder-driven initiatives.

Up to this point, I've used the words "leader" and "founder" more or less interchangeably. But I'd like to distinguish between the two because, while related, the two are not synonymous. All good founders are leaders, but all leaders are not necessarily founders. A startup founder will zero in on a business idea, create the necessary business structure, pitch investors, recruit team members, and produce goods or services. A leader might join that same company a few years down the road and expand its product line and globalize its offerings. The latter is integral to the company's success, but she's not necessarily a founder.

Let's put it in a kid's perspective: A founder organizes hiking parties and starts new school initiatives. A leader is elected student body president and improves upon the system that is already in place. Both are valuable roles, but they are different. That's not to say that leaders don't inspire people. A CEO won't last long in her position if her colleagues and employees aren't confident in her vision for her company and its future. But founders must rally people around their missions from day one, often before they can prove that an idea makes sense or is achievable.

In other words, founders create something that did not previously exist. That might be a company, social organization, a team with a cause, or a one-time event. The opportunities to found are limitless, but they're all defined by the fact that they revolve around starting something new. The skill set necessary to become a founder is a superset of those required to be a leader. But the core trait of founders is the ability to inspire others to follow you.

In this chapter, we'll explore this and other attributes common to effective founders. We'll also talk about ways you can nurture your children's founder-like instincts, from putting a positive spin on conversations to vision-writing sessions.

The 3 Traits of Great Founders

While no two founders will be exactly alike, bringing an idea into reality requires a few key characteristics. These are:

Inspirational Character

The most effective founders are consumed by passion and enthusiasm for their ideas. When they talk to you about their ideas for a world-changing product or for a school fundraiser that will transform the student experience, you can't help but get caught up in the excitement. Their energy—along with their Founder's Top Three—creates a wave that sweeps up everyone in their path until they have a team of people dedicated to their cause.

It's that excitement that helps get other people interested; as people learn about what founders are creating, how they're creating it, and why they're tackling this project in the first place, they're naturally drawn to the project. That's how I like to operate, and it's what I've taught Annie and Blake to do as well. Then you're not hard-selling people on your concept; you've already got them excited with their own emotional enthusiasm. The conversation shifts from "Would you like to join me?" to "I'm so glad to hear you're interested. Here's how we're doing this." Instead of imposing ideas on another person, founders are channeling momentum established by others' interest and desire to be a part of a team or contribute to an idea, cause, or business.

I witnessed this with Annie as she pursued scaling her Bear Cubs Running Team organization that she founded at Washington University in St. Louis into a national movement. As I shared earlier in this book, Annie was deeply moved when she met a friend's sister who loved running, but the girl was not able to run on school teams because of the limitations that autism created. Annie started the group locally when she was in high school and expanded on the concept when she got to college and began running at a collegiate level. She rallied teammates and peers from other universities around her mission to make team running accessible to student athletes who are on the autism spectrum. Now she has people approaching her asking for help to start their own chapters. It's an incredible story of founding in action, and it proves that kids can be incredibly effective when given the proper support.

Drive

Ideas alone don't spark passionate followings; they have to be attended to. In Christopher Nolan's 2010 film *Inception*, Leonardo DiCaprio's character says, "Once an idea has taken hold of the brain, it's almost impossible to eradicate. An idea that is fully formed—fully understood—that sticks, right in there somewhere." What does that mean for founding? Lots of people have great ideas all the time, but founders take that idea and hold on to it, make it stick, and make it a reality.

That takes *drive*. (And this is where our concept of banning negative words reappears.) Founders don't let good ideas pass through their minds without a second thought. They wrestle with ideas and embrace their nemesis, even when those nasty instances of "can't be done" and "impossible" creep up. When a good idea hits, great founders know not to let obstacles get in the way.

"Founders don't let good ideas pass through their minds without a second thought."

Action

The final essential quality is action; founders *always* channel their passion into a plan with action. Inspiration and drive—no matter how tenacious—only go so far without real steps put into place. Action doesn't always have to be huge, share-worthy efforts, though many mistakenly think that it does. A lot of the time (and especially early on), action means small steps. It might be reaching out to a friend who knows more about what you're trying to do or simply setting aside a few afternoons with Google to discover more about a subject.

But those small steps inevitably build momentum. The more you learn about an idea you have, the more you spend time with it (whether it's a nemesis you're embracing or a friendly idea you're running along with), the more you're building it up. That, in turn, helps founders exhibit the other two traits: You have more drive behind the idea, and you have more of a reason to get excited about it and recruit others to help.

Teaching Your Children to Found

We went over this in the introduction, but it's been a while, so let me reiterate: If you haven't founded a company or don't work in the business field, you may feel you have little to impart to your children about becoming founders. But that simply isn't true. No matter what your professional background, within your past, you hold rich life experiences from which your children can learn. Every time you've successfully hosted a family reunion or holiday dinner, you founded an event. The monthly book club for moms that you organize or the dads-only running group that you corral every Saturday morning? Those are founding successes, too. You had an idea, brought it to life, and got people excited about it. That takes skills, ones your children can learn a great deal from.

The following strategies will help you shape your kids' thinking and draw on your own wisdom to teach them the essential traits of a founder.

1. Emphasize action, no matter how big the problem.

It's very easy to dwell on the problems in the world without progressing toward solutions. There's comfort in gathering around the dinner table each evening and commiserating about the fearful state of society. But harping on negativity is a cognitive trap. Remember that the words we use change our brains. The same principles that underscore my rule about banning "can't" and "impossible" apply to negative conversations. I'm not suggesting that you put blinders on to what's happening around you. But I caution against discussing those problems with your kids without including a positive upshot or a real-life, actionable application to solving those problems.

When my family circles around an upsetting issue and the phrase "shouldn't be that way" crops up, I stop and ask what we're going to do about it. If we're expending time and mental energy discussing it, then let's take positive action toward a solution, rather than dwelling (falling into a victim mentality) and redeclaring why things "shouldn't be that way," with the unspoken statement "It's unfair." Such discussion presents a great opportunity to practice finding the PTS. You're not likely to end global terrorism or solve the climate crisis over a Wednesday evening dinner, but at the very least, you can distinguish the actual problems from the ostensible. You can invite your kids to share their thoughts on why people have such strong emotional reactions to these crises and how they might personally approach conversations with others more effectively based on those insights.

Perhaps these discussions will spark ideas for how your kids can take action in their own lives. Or maybe they'll plant a seed of interest that will one day blossom into a meaningful career. The important thing is that you shift from an atmosphere of negativity and passivity to one of positivity and action. Your kids will then learn to make this shift in other areas of their lives. When Blake was invited to be a staff member at the Boy Scouts leadership training mentioned in the last chapter, he was honored by the opportunity. But he was also dismayed by the inefficiencies and gaps he saw in the program. Instead of complaining, however, he wrote thoughtful recommendations for how the training could be improved. His ideas were well-received, and he was given the chance to train his senior trainers in the new methods. MJ and I were extremely proud of him for working to make something better instead of stewing in frustration.

2. Hold vision-writing sessions.

Putting pen to paper is an extremely powerful way to clarify your vision. Whenever our kids got excited about a new idea, MJ and I encouraged them to grab a notebook and flesh out the concepts in writing. We also encouraged Blake and Annie to write out their Rocking Chair Retrospectives (RCRs), mentioned earlier in this book. What would success look like for each goal? How would they feel once they achieved these milestones? Starting with the desired outcome frees you from second-guessing yourself or attempting to plan the steps to these outcomes as you're documenting them. If you start with writing the steps it will take to get there, you might abandon the project because it seems too difficult. But if you can see the endpoint clearly, you will then be more likely to unlock the steps and find a way to make your RCR real.

An RCR, or future retrospective, isn't unheard of among founders—this has helped me win sales contracts and investor funding multiple times, and the CEO of Rival Theory, a company of which I am chairman, shared recently that writing his RCR helped him obtain a considerable amount of funding and partnership interest in his business. As for another example, pre-writing a press release is a common tactic taught in business schools, and it's regularly used by product managers at Amazon.[1]

I regularly encourage, and sometimes require, young entrepreneurs asking for my assistance to write their RCRs. When they are struggling too much with immediate issues or are too locked to a short-term growth plan and may not be willing to see the future implications of their short-term views, I will engage them in this exercise. Research shows that entrepreneurs who write down their strategies and document their plans are significantly more likely to succeed than those who don't.[2] Whether your children start a business or become community activists, the habit of writing out their goals, or pre-writing their successes, will prove crucial to realizing their dreams.

3. Encourage more positive attitudes.

We touched on this in the last chapter, but it bears repeating because founders do not wallow in failure. If you want your kids to be confident in themselves, you can't make excuses for them, nor can you allow them to do so. Dismissing failure as a shortcoming on the coach's or teacher's part disempowers your children. You're telling them that they're victims, and that identity will shape their choices throughout their lives.

Instead of focusing on negativity and victimhood, teach your children to see failure as an opportunity to move in a new direction. This transforms the conversation. Rehashing disappointments and injustices creates a negative feedback loop that is very hard to break. Identifying opportunities amid the setbacks injects hope and positivity.

4. Help kids pivot when necessary.

For founders, pivoting from an original idea to one that works better is almost inevitable. I've been here myself many times. Shortly after founding Eyefluence, I came to the unsettling realization that we didn't have a market for our initial product. I had to go to our stakeholders and tell them we needed to overhaul our business plan and go in an entirely different direction. It was embarrassing and disheartening. But rather than stew in those feelings or blame our consultants, I asked, "What else can we do with this technology?" That question vastly broadened our opportunities.

There's a big difference between failing and pivoting. Helping your kids make the distinction will be critical to honing their founder sensibilities. No matter how great an idea your child has, someone will push back against it. People resist change, and unfortunately, they often discount kids' ideas. The skill to learn in these moments is distinguishing between baseless naysaying and a signal to adjust, adapt, or pivot.

This is an area in which your own experience can be quite beneficial. Whether you're an entrepreneur doesn't matter. I have no doubt that you have both founded and pivoted on ideas many times in your life. Share these experiences with your kids. They'll learn by understanding your thought process and realize that it's OK to pivot or to let go of projects when they're not viable.

As parents, we are reluctant to show vulnerability. We want to be strong for our kids at all times. But sometimes being strong means being vulnerable. And we don't do our kids any favors when we pretend that nothing bothers us. When they see us as human, they see that it's OK for them to have problems and failures, too. They also feel more comfortable sharing their frustrations because they know their pain falls on sympathetic ears.

5. Stack success.

No matter how many achievements you reach in life, starting a new initiative can seem daunting. You question whether you can reach your goals, whether you can raise the money, and whether people will follow you. Even though you've developed the necessary skills and have a proven record of success, you will still encounter doubts and fears.

You'll see this often with your kids. They'll win an award at school or succeed in a project they started. But when the next opportunity arises, they'll get nervous. Was the first time a fluke? Are they really smart enough or strong enough to win again? The steeper the challenge, the more likely they are to default to the "I can't do this" position. But as we know, "can't" is inadmissible. Instead, talk to your kids about their past achievements. List the different skills and strategies they used to reach that goal. Then, talk about how those same skills and strategies will apply to this new project. This will help your child connect the threads and see that future success builds on past achievement. And past achievements show a pattern of success that suggest that future success is, indeed, possible. Then your kids will feel more self-assured as they approach new challenges, feeling confident that success is in their control, not something that's left up to chance.

6. Involve your children in your endeavors.

Just as parents often assume their kids aren't interested in their work, they apply the same mentality to other areas of their lives. You might think, "Why would my kids care about the fundraiser I'm organizing for the PTA or the dinner I'm planning for Saturday night?" Because you're their parent! Everything you do is fascinating to your kids, if you share it with enthusiasm and contextualize it in terms that they understand, especially when they're young. If they're not interested, you can be sure they'll let you know, and then you can determine whether you've taken your best shot at making it interesting to them. But give them the chance to decide—and keep coming back, asking them again and again to join you in some endeavor. More often than not, your children will want to be as involved as you'll allow, and if you begin this involvement when they are young, they'll more likely engage even when they reach teen years.

Talk to your kids about the events you're organizing and even personal projects you do in your spare time. Openly grapple with whether a car wash, bake sale, or VR-a-Thon will be a more effective fundraiser. Wonder aloud how to increase attendance at this year's talent show. Tell them where you're stuck with a painting or short story. Then, listen to their feedback. Who knows? Kids are extremely creative, and a simple comment from them might shake a new idea loose. As they grow, if you listen carefully, they will absolutely help you solve problems.

Bring your children along to meetings about different events and ask their opinions about what happened. Explain your objectives beforehand, then ask for feedback afterward. Engaging them shows that you respect their opinions, which bolsters their confidence in sharing their ideas. As kids get older, encourage them to participate in meetings as well. Your kids may pick up on cues and details that you miss. I've been in meetings in which Annie interjected, and my first instinct was to hush her so as not to put an investor or client off. But she had actually integrated the concepts we were discussing in a succinct and insightful way, and the speaker excitedly riffed on her remarks. That's a win in both parenting and business, and it can happen across a wide spectrum of circumstances.

As the most influential person in your children's lives, you can help them see problems through a different lens. Here's a story that illustrates this: Blake has long been passionate about environmentalism and human health (you may recall that it was Annie, not Blake, who needed some convincing about swearing off partially hydrogenated oils). When he became an Eagle Scout, he decided to rally his troop around water conservation. He reached out to the local utility company to little avail. He left messages for three weeks but couldn't get a call back.

Blake assumed the utility company wasn't interested, but I posed an alternative possibility. I knew firsthand that a lack of response is often due to limited time and resources rather than disinterest. I received many interesting pitches but simply didn't have the capacity to respond to them all. So Blake and I did some brainstorming. How might he change his approach? He called the utility department again, but this time he left a detailed message explaining how his Eagle Scout troop was interested in helping distribute the public utility's water conservation kits deeper into our home county. That got the department's attention. By repositioning the request to describe how the Scouts would help the utility—not just offer a vague (albeit well-intentioned) ability to help—he addressed its need specifically and motivated someone to call him back. Had Blake not confided his struggle to me, he might have assumed that no response meant no interest and abandoned the effort. But I have more business and life experience, so I was able to get inside the utility leaders' minds and help him see a different way of approaching them.

You can do this for your children, as well, in a variety of situations. If their friends aren't on board with a club they've started or outing they've planned, you can help them empathize with that reluctance. How can your children present the idea in a way that appeals to other people? Blake and I also discussed how he would keep his Scout buddies motivated to give up their free time to distribute water conservation kits to strangers. The first time out, he offered free pizza for anyone who volunteered, but only a handful of Scouts showed up. We talked about tying the activity to a more motivating value instead. At subsequent Scout meetings, Blake explained how many ounces of water they could help people save each month and the effect that would have over the next several years. Offering a way to make a concrete difference was far more effective in motivating his fellow Scouts than dangling a couple of free slices of pizza in front of them.

Sometimes we get so caught up in our own ideas that we forget everyone else isn't on board yet; we don't know how to get them to connect with our passions. You've had a lot more time to practice empathy and understand what's going on in other people's lives, and that's an incredibly valuable skill to model for your future founders.

Tools, Fun, & Magic Moments

Once you know where to look, you'll find endless ways to teach your kids how to found. Here are a few suggestions for inspiring budding founders through common family activities:

1. Get involved in your kids' school projects.

Science projects in particular are great opportunities to engage with your kids. Teachers usually constrain students' options, making these assignments ideal moments to talk about being creative within constraints or breaking the rules to create a better outcome. If your child struggles with science and feels overwhelmed by the project, you can come back to the problem to solve (PTS). What's the purpose of the assignment? What is the teacher hoping to see from these projects? Perhaps your child needs to schedule a one-on-one consultation with the teacher to better understand the assignment. Each step along the path allows you to guide your child through questions and empathy without stepping in and doing the work for him. Because frustrations are inevitable during big projects, you'll likely have the opportunity to help your child practice shifting from negative to positive thinking as well.

2. Found something together.

What better way to bond with your kids than starting something together? When Annie and I decided to bake our own cookies for her Girl Scout troop, we had the wonderful opportunity of founding something alongside one another—and there are countless opportunities for any family to do the same. You can organize a neighborhood block party, start a parent-child running team, or petition the local government to improve security at your nearby park. If you're a creative family, you might start a band together or collaborate on an artistic endeavor. The options are limitless, so have fun with this! Founding something together allows you and your children to learn from one another and to deepen your relationship by working through challenges and experiencing triumphs and setbacks together.

3. Let the kids take the lead on a family activity.

This one is more than just ordering for themselves at a restaurant or navigating in the car. Give your children ownership over an activity or event. Let them run with their ideas and experience what it's like to pitch an idea and drum up enthusiasm for it. If you take an annual vacation, ask your older children to choose a location and decide where you'll stay and what you'll see there. To avoid disappointment, you may want to put some parameters on this, such as how far away you can afford to travel and a nightly budget for hotels. But give them the freedom to fill in the details. For younger kids, you might start smaller, such as letting them plan the agenda for a Friday family night. Brainstorming and executing on big ideas does wonders for kids' creativity and confidence.

This development of independence led to a recent heartwarming development in our family. Blake considered Annie's interests and his own experiences in traveling, and for Annie's graduation gift from college, he gave her a prepaid ticket to travel, round trip, to any location in the world. I consider this an aspect of "founding" and reinforcing a lifelong bond between two siblings.

A Closing Note

I hope it's clear by now that founding is about so much more than starting companies. It's about running with your passions and ideas and learning to translate those into action. And parents are incredible founders, but they don't always see themselves as such. I think MJ put it best when she said that people aren't born leaders and founders—they grow into these roles based on the lessons they learn early in life. That's what we have aimed to do with our children and what we hope we can share with your family.

When MJ and I were discussing the ideas I'd share in this book, she emphasized that we're not a perfect family. We don't have it all figured out, and just because we're proud of the people Blake and Annie have become doesn't mean we don't worry about them. That never stops, no matter how old or mature or successful your children are. But MJ told me that she believes our family works because we always come back to compassion and humility. As long as we are empathizing with other people and are willing to get up and pursue our missions each day, we can consider ourselves founders. And that is a mindset that is within every child's, and every parent's, reach.

Conclusion

By this point, I hope you feel inspired to embrace your inner founder and empowered to raise your children to be the bright, world-changing founders and leaders you know they have the potential to be. It's been a pleasure for me to share what I've learned as an entrepreneur and as a father of two founders, and I hope you've found my family's stories insightful.

You've heard a lot about my family throughout Blake and Annie's childhood, and to put together everything you've read, here's a quick look at where we are now:

Blake, now 25, is the founder and CEO of Epharmix, a digital healthcare company that facilitates automated communications between patients and their healthcare providers. Epharmix is only a few years old, but it's already making an impact—the team has had research accepted by the Society for Academic Emergency Medicine and is partnering with local hospitals to decrease unnecessary patient readmission. Blake was also included in the St. Louis Business Journal's 30 Under 30 list in 2015.

Annie is 23, and she is looking at how she might expand the Bear Cubs Running Team into a national organization—at the time of writing this, she's already in talks with individuals and organizations interested in supporting her vision. Keep in mind that the precursor to Bear Cubs started as more of an informal idea of hers when she was in high school; she simply wanted to include her friend's younger sister in athletics, not start a national organization. It was her ability to recognize an evolving PTS that took her from square one to where she is now.

MJ, a pilot, has published articles and books on her flying stories, is a speaker at aviation events, and has trained for suborbital space flight. And note that she began this journey at the age of 45—simply because she wanted to. Most recently, she began pursuing her doctorate from the University of Southern California's School of Education in Organizational Change and Leadership to address issues in long-duration space travel.

As for me, I'm a founder at heart and continue to sprinkle, nourish, or drive ideas that affect people. I speak and advise individuals and companies, and I found events, businesses, and organizations focused on world-improving causes. I'm currently exploring a new idea to use AI to improve human connectedness. I am on the board of Oblong Industries, a collaboration technology company, supporting its CEO and founder, John Underkoffler, who created Tom Cruise's iconic HCI (human-computer interaction) scene in *Minority Report*. I advise Foresight AI and Rival Theory, which use artificial intelligence to improve the human condition through mobile robotic data and AI personas, respectively. I'm on the board of directors for Team Gleason, a foundation that aims to improve the lives of ALS patients, and I counsel numerous other startups and entrepreneurs. I am a Rotary member of the Lamorinda Sunrise Rotary Club and recently founded a project with Rotary International addressing peace and polio—the world's first VR-a-Thon, a fundraising effort where Rotary hosts raise money through sponsorship of short, emotive VR content viewed through smartphones and VR headsets.

Before we close, I'd like to return once more to the idea of the Rocking Chair Retrospective (RCR), because it truly is important for not only having a founder's mindset, but also for creating something valuable using that mindset. There's no better way to clarify your goals and dreams than to work backward from the end of your life and identify what truly matters to you. But the real beauty of this exercise is that it helps you envision and realize your achievement of those milestones.

The best founders, and the best parents, know they can't always control what happens to them. But they can decide how they'll respond and how they'll conduct themselves day to day to mitigate disappointment as much as possible. Writing your RCR will help bring the essence of what really matters to you to light.

I know many business executives who create future retrospectives for milestones in their companies. Executives zero in on a goal, such as reaching a particular sales number, launching a new product, or achieving explicit annual targets. But for the purposes of this book, I'd like you to think in broader terms. Imagine that you're in your twilight years, and you're sitting in a rocking chair on your front porch. Perhaps the sun is setting on a gentle spring day, and you find yourself lost in rumination about your lifelong journey. Your thoughts circle around three questions:

- What did you enjoy most in your life?
- What are you most proud of?
- How did you most contribute?

I encourage you to really spend time with these questions. Pick a distant age—80, 100, 120—and write your answers as though you are rocking in your chair *at that age*. Looking back over your life, when you answer these questions, consider what type of person, and what type of parent, you became. Be specific. Write, "I remember when I…." Are there things you did with your children that you enjoyed or are proud of? What did you do to contribute to them, friends, others, or the world? Did you write a novel? Or did you start a company? Did you travel the world volunteering with your family? Did you win a Nobel Prize or save the life of a person in need? Did you sculpt a statue for your grandchildren? What values did you instill in your children?

Put everything on the table. Tell your story, from the future. The more clearly you describe the life you lived, the more you'll understand yourself and your priorities now, and the more likely that you will take some journey that embraces those ideas—whether you achieve the specific listed outcomes or not.

I'll warn you that this can be a frightening exercise, not just because you're imagining the end of your life, but because it forces you to confront your deepest dreams and fears. In my experience, however, a more emotional and frightening process leads to a richer outcome.

Once you've seen the past from the future and considered your values, beliefs, hopes, and ambitions, ask yourself, "What behaviors am I going to adopt to create these outcomes *now*?" RCRs are emotionally motivating, but they won't get you very far without the next step—a plan and action. Identify the tools you'll need, the social and familial support, the education, the professional training—anything you think will be required on the journey.

Then get out there and live it. The greatest gift you can give your children is living thoughtfully and with integrity because you'll teach them to do the same. Raising a founder takes courage, and it will challenge you in ways you never imagined.

But the rewards are immense. And you now have this book to guide you on your journey.

Nothing in the world matters more to parents than their children achieving their fullest potential. As we've talked about in these pages, developing a founder's mindset isn't always easy for parents or kids. But with the many incredible experiences to be shared along the way, you will be truly humbled by the innovations, kindnesses, gratitude, and meaning your children will bring to the world.

During the next months and years, I hope you'll return to the stories and activities in this book and see which ones resonate with your family. Some of the greatest joys in my life have occurred while playing The Restaurant Game or doing silly word puzzles with Blake and Annie. And some of my most profound conversations have been spent talking through tough problems with MJ and our kids. I believe that all parents have the capacity to create those experiences with their children, and I hope you, too, experience deep joy and fulfillment in your family's founders' journeys!

Sources

Not only did these concepts work for my family—but they're also backed by studies, statistics, and other examples. Here, you'll find the resources we used to ensure this book's ideas are ones proven in the world:

Chapter 1

1. "Are You Trying to Solve the Wrong Problem?" by Peter Bregman. Published in Harvard Business Review, December 7, 2015. https://hbr.org/2015/12/are-you-solving-the-wrong-problem
2. "China's Numbers Are Shorter Than Ours" by Robert Krulwich. Published on NPR, July 1, 2011. http://www.npr.org/sections/krulwich/2011/07/01/137527742/china-s-unnatural-math-advantage-their-words
3. "Cognitive Development in Children: Piaget" by Jean Piaget. Published in the Journal of Research in Science Teaching,

Volume 2, September 1964. http://onlinelibrary.wiley.com/doi/10.1002/tea.3660020306/full

4. "I Keep Six Honest Serving-Men" by Rudyard Kipling. Published on KiplingSociety.co.uk. http://www.kiplingsociety.co.uk/poems_serving.htm

5. "Final Determination Regarding Partially Hydrogenated Oils." Published by U.S. Food and Drug Administration, January 1, 2018. https://www.fda.gov/food/ingredientspackaginglabeling/foodadditivesingredients/ucm449162.htm

Chapter 2

1. "Americans Falter on Geography Test." Published in The New York Times, July 28, 1988. http://www.nytimes.com/1988/07/28/us/americans-falter-on-geography-test.html

2. "National Geography Standards and Skills." Published on National Geographic. https://www.nationalgeographic.org/education/national-geography-standards/

3. "Childhood stimulation key to brain development, study finds" by Alok Jha. Published in The Guardian, October 14, 2012. https://www.theguardian.com/science/2012/oct/14/childhood-stimulation-key-brain-development

4. "The lasting impact of neglect" by Kirsten Weir. Published in the Monitor on Psychology, Volume 45, No. 6, June 2014. http://www.apa.org/monitor/2014/06/neglect.aspx

5. "The Power of Talking to Your Baby" by Tina Rosenberg. Published in The New York Times Opinionator, April 10, 2013. https://opinionator.blogs.nytimes.com/2013/04/10/the-power-of-talking-to-your-baby/

6. "The Importance of Talking to Babies" by Alice Sterling Honig. Published on Scholastic. http://www.scholastic.com/browse/article.jsp?id=893

7. *The New First Three Years of Life* by Burton L. White. Published August 1, 1995.

8. "Why You Should Do Nothing When Your Child Says, 'I'm Bored'" by Dr. Vanessa Lapointe. Published on HuffPost, December 6, 2017. https://www.huffingtonpost.com/dr-vanessa-lapointe/why-you-should-do-nothing_b_9818144.html

9. "The development of metacognitive ability in adolescence" by Leonora G. Weil et. al. Published in Consciousness and Cognition, Volume 22, Issue 1, March 2013. http://www.sciencedirect.com/science/article/pii/S1053810013000068

10. "Why Do Our Best Ideas Come in the Shower?" by Lucas Reilly. Published on Mental Floss, September 6, 2013. http://mentalfloss.com/article/52586/why-do-our-best-ideas-come-us-shower

11. "10 challenges of being an accountant" by Rachel Allen. Published on Clear Books, October 22, 2015. https://www.clearbooks.co.uk/blog/10-challenges-of-being-an-accountant/

Chapter 3

1. "The Sequoia 'RIP: Good Times' presentation: Here it is" by Eric Eldon. Published in VentureBeat, October 10, 2008. https://venturebeat.com/2008/10/10/the-sequoia-rip-good-times-presentation-get-your-copy-here/

2. *The Medici Effect: What Elephants and Epidemics Can Teach Us About Innovation* by Frans Johansson. Published October 1,

2006.
3. "Biomimetic Architecture: Green Building in Zimbabwe Modeled After Termite Mounds" by Abigail Doan. Published on inhabitat, November 29, 2012. http://inhabitat.com/building-modelled-on-termites-eastgate-centre-in-zimbabwe/

Chapter 4

1. *What the Face Reveals: Basic and Applied Studies of Spontaneous Expression Using the Facial Action Coding System (FACS)*, Second Edition by Paul Ekman and Erika L. Rosenberg. Published by Oxford University Press, 2005.
2. "Left Brain, Right Brain? Wrong" by Stephen M. Kosslyn, PhD, and G. Wayne Miller. Published in Psychology Today, January 27, 2014. https://www.psychologytoday.com/blog/the-theory-cognitive-modes/201401/left-brain-right-brain-wrong
3. "My stroke of insight" by Jill Bolte Taylor. Recorded at TED2008, February 2008.
4. "The End of Rational Vs. Emotional: How Both Logic and Feeling Play Key Roles in Marketing and Decision-Making" by Douglas Van Praet. Published in Fast Company, May 16, 2013. https://www.fastcompany.com/1682962/the-end-of-rational-vs-emotional-how-both-logic-and-feeling-play-key-roles-in-marketing-and-
5. "Thinking, Fast and Slow" by Daniel Kahneman. Published April 2, 2013.
6. "Your body language may shape who you are" by Amy Cuddy. Recorded at TEDGlobal 2012, June 2012. https://www.ted.com/talks/amy_cuddy_your_body_language_shapes_who_

you_are?language=en
7. "Reading literary fiction improves empathy, study finds" by Liz Bury. Published on The Guardian, October 8, 2013. https://www.theguardian.com/books/booksblog/2013/oct/08/literary-fiction-improves-empathy-study

Chapter 5

1. *Queen Bees and Wannabes: Helping Your Daughter Survive Cliques, Gossip, Boyfriends, and the New Realities of Girl World* by Rosalind Wiseman. Published October 13, 2009.
2. "The language of parenting: Legitimacy of parental authority" by Nancy Darling, PhD. Published in Psychology Today, January 11, 2010. https://www.psychologytoday.com/blog/thinking-about-kids/201001/the-language-parenting-legitimacy-parental-authority
3. "Power Causes Brain Damage" by Jerry Useem. Published in The Atlantic, July/August 2017. https://www.theatlantic.com/magazine/archive/2017/07/power-causes-brain-damage/528711/
4. "The scientific explanation for why so many CEOs act like jerks" by Nick Tasler. Published on Quartz, June 27, 2017. https://qz.com/1015215/do-ceos-have-to-be-nice-now/
5. "Trust-Building Exercises for Kids" by Ann Bartkowski. Published on Livestrong, May 5, 2013. http://www.livestrong.com/article/210884-trust-building-exercises-for-kids/

Chapter 6

1. "Why Amazon forces its developers to write press releases" by Jillian D'Onfro. Published on Business Insider, March 12, 2015. http://www.businessinsider.com/heres-the-surprising-way-amazon-decides-what-new-enterprise-products-to-work-on-next-2015-3
2. "Research: Writing a Business Plan Makes Your Startup More Likely to Succeed" by Francis J. Greene and Christian Hopp. Published on Harvard Business Review, July 14, 2017. https://hbr.org/2017/07/research-writing-a-business-plan-makes-your-startup-more-likely-to-succeed

Photos

Jim's undergraduate graduation from MIT in 1980

Annie and Blake in 1998, preschool and first grade

Top: Blake and Annie, ages 12 and 10, at Jim's "Father of the Year" award ceremony in 2004
Bottom: MJ, Jim, and Blake at the "Father of the Year" award ceremony in 2004

Our family members and their passions in 2005: Annie's long-distance running leading to Bear Cubs and social entrepreneurship; MJ taking flight with VFR, IFR, CFR, and CFI ratings leading to international Gravity Games with Students for Space Exploration and Development; Jim's award-winning LeapFrog Fly Pentop invention, which lead to Livescribe and Eyefluence; and Blake's taekwondo physical and mental training, which led to his black belt, Eagle Scouts, ISEF, BetaVersity, and Epharmix.

Top: Blake and Jim hiking in Yosemite in 2009

Right: Blake measuring out ratios of chemicals on an improvised "spoon scale" for making gunpowder in sixth grade

Top Left: Annie as a high school sophomore in 2011 following her passion — distance running!
Top Right: Blake laden with Boy Scout badges at his Eagle Scout award ceremony as a sophomore in high school
Bottom: Family outing in 2010: MJ, Annie, Jim, and Blake

Top: Co-inventors Blake and Matt Feddersen with Jay Chugh, their high school science teacher, at the 2011 Intel Science and Engineering Fair ahead of Blake and Matt winning The Gordon E. Moore Award

Bottom: Blake and friends at Blake's first garage startup, PackSay, in summer 2012

Top: Annie after finishing eighth at the 2012
California Interscholastic Federation Division
III State Cross Country Championships

Bottom: Annie wearing EyeCom glasses in 2012
prior to Jim founding Eyefluence

Top: Blake and Jim at Blake's high school graduation

Bottom: Jim, Annie, and MJ at Annie's high school graduation in 2013

Acknowledgments

Writing a book—especially one about parenting and being a founder—isn't a solitary endeavor. Thanks to my wife, MJ, and our children, Blake and Annie, for providing the life experiences and memories that fill this book and for supporting me as I wrote it. And thanks to the following individuals who have influenced me, my career, and the ideas found in this book:

From my days at Eyefluence: my co-founders Dave Stiehr and Peter Milford, and team members, investors, and Board members, Eliot Drake, Michelle Hodgden, Rob Rohm, Nate Penrod, Chris Spitler, Angel Kano, John Bird, Sam McMullen IV, Larry Udell, Nelson Publicover, Bill Torch, Randy Haykin, Spencer Connaughton, James Darpinian, Tom DuBois, Andy Hartzell, Ben Holman, Bo Hu, Vlad Ivanchenko, Gurmeet Kalra, David Karr, Nikhil Khare, Clayton Kimber, Peter Lambert, Ray Lee, Nathan Lord, David Lively, Luke Lu, Kristen Lurie, Stefan Lynggaard, Zoe Meraz, Scott Martin, David Merkoski, Steve Mitchell, Michael Montvelishsky, Rory Pierce, Sergey Prokushkin, Michael Santoro, Sherri Schultz-Ramos, Steve Stolper, Raz Turiac, Elizabeth Weber, Zhaoyi Wei, Thomas

Craven-Bartle, Mats Petter Wallander, Petter Erricsson, Yohan Baillot, Debra Rosen, Jesse Davis, Peter Diamandis, Mark Stevens, Bill English, Sam McMullen Jr., John Spinale, Rob Rueckert, Charlie Melcher, Roger Ohanesian, Paul Weinstein, Woo Kim, David Dolby, Pascal Levensohn, Andrew Krowne, Mark Jones, Randall Jones, Bart Jones, Steve Jones, Steve and Paula Schwartz, Nick Wechsler, Gary Riske, Rick Intrater, Brandon Intrater, Jesse Wellen, Don Jenkins, Chuck Bove, David Waal, Thomas Raeth, Hays Englehart, Daryl Drake, and Matt Chaney—all of whom helped me continue to refine my founding skills.

Through great times and challenging moments at Livescribe: Sasha Pesic, Byron Connell, Helen Thomas, Holly DeLeon, Marc Thomas, Dinesh Raghavan, Ken Cucarola, Frank Lucero, Frank Canova, Eric Petitt, Chris Cast, TC Edgecomb, Rohan Marr, Gopalakrishnan Cary, Joe Khleif, Linda McFarland, Andy Van Schaack, Barry McQuain, Nagraj Kashyap, Jay Eum, Mike Stark, Rory O'Driscoll, Cynthia Ringo, David Hartford, Örjan Johansson, Stein Revelsby, the larger Livescribe team, and our investors and board members.

Through explosive growth and impact at LeapFrog: Mike Wood, Bob Lally, Tim Bender, Jessie Woolley-Wilson, Madeline Schroeder, Matt Brown, Tom Kalinske, Karen Fuson, Keith Stanovich, Anne Cunningham, Ruth Nathan, Suzy Schuman, Warren Buckleitner, Miguel Helft, Clive Thompson, and hundreds of other committed friends and associates.

During early founding days at StrataCom: Pete Stonebridge, David Owen, Charles Corbalis, Bill Stensrud, Dick Moley, Scott Kriens, Steve Campbell, Gaymond Schultz, Jon Masatsugu, Mark Vatuone, Mike Ernst, Brian Button, Matt Powell, Rick Pfleger, Alan Greenfield, Mark Watson, Alex Mendez, Sanjay Subhedar, Steven Haley, Preston Kilman, Dan Kosek, Mike

Levender, Kambiz Hooshmand, Brian Holden, Geof Kirsch, Peter Alexander, Vernon Brokke, Deborah Flanagan, Chris Sommers, Randy Presuhn, Steve Montoya, Rick Landsman, Mike Matthys, Sunil Dhar, Clyde Iwamoto, Chris Helfer, and colleagues from engineering, marketing, sales, support, manufacturing, and finance.

From Explore Technologies: my co-founders and friends, Mark Flowers and Dave Conroy, David Brewer, Joe Khirallah, Rick Adolf, Larry Lynch, Tom Musolf, Roger Bergen, Dick Voell, Fred Brownson, and an amazing pioneering team.

My formative short stay at ROLM: Richard Faubert, Barbara Van Remortel, Keith Meehan, Leslie Meehan, Denise Teske, Glen Riley, Kevin McPartlan, Jim Von De Bur, and other friends exploring adventures in our twenties.

Friends who sparked my entrepreneurial, founding spirit in my college years: Nghia Van Nguyen, Bob Strunce, Dan Douglas, Murray Biggs, Charlie Frankel, Rich Byrne, Bill Brown, Tom Woolfolk, Tim Morgenthaler, Tom Neu, Jay White, Charlie Freeman, Tom Vasicek, and many other fraternity brothers from the Massachusetts Gamma Chapter of Phi Delta Theta and friends from the MIT Shakespeare Ensemble and the MIT community.

Some powerfully influential teachers and friends from Shepaug Valley Regional High School who had a major influence on my education and outlook in life: Blanche Bailey, Bob Hopkins, Jack Miller, Don Giroux, Cyrus Miller, Keith Miller, Wendy Miller, Chapin Miller, and Clay Squire.

Friends, founders, and thinkers with whom I have had many spirited entrepreneurial discussions through the years, including Dan Fraisl, Carey Rappaport, Frank Vallese, and Bob Allen.

Inspiring people whose lives, and the discussions we've had, have inspired me to reach well beyond myself: Steve Gleason,

Mike Milken, Peter Diamandis, Walt Mossberg, and Tony Robbins.

Rotarians in our Lamorinda Sunrise Club; at Rotary International Headquarters in Evanston, Illinois; and the larger Rotary and Rotaractor community around the world.

Family members who have offered support: Marcia, Brian, Megan, and Connor Mitchell; Russ Pratt; Janet and Gene Savickas; Fred and Maureen Gustafson; Andy and Ginny Napolitano; Elaine Babiyon; and my mom and dad, Mary Ann and Pete, who are no longer with us.

The team at Influence & Co., including Joanie Zinser, Elle Hammond, Seanna Tucker, and Carolina VonKampen.

About the Author

Jim Marggraff is a serial entrepreneur who is dedicated to developing innovative technologies that improve learning and productivity. He is the founder and CEO of Eyefluence, a company that transforms intent into action by leveraging eye biomechanics and the eye-brain connection to create an eye-interaction technology solution for head-mounted displays. Eyefluence was recently acquired by Google. Jim has founded or co-founded several successful companies, including Livescribe, Explore Technologies, and StrataCom. He invented the LeapFrog LeapPad Learning System, leading to sales of more than $1 billion worldwide, and the Livescribe smartpen, both of which help students and adults around the world. Jim holds at least 36 pending and accepted patents, and he is listed as one of MIT's top 150 inventors.

Jim and his wife, MJ, live in California, and they are the parents of two founders in their own right, Blake and Annie.